"In a world where "eve[...] in his own eyes," Dr. [...] [...]-pelling, and biblical c[...] [...] restoration of strong fatherly roles in the church. In our generation, we have many instructors, but fathers are woefully deficient. The nation of Israel was under judgement when children and babes were their rulers. *Where Have All the Fathers Gone* is a timely and much needed book for believers in our generation. Our churches and nation will be blessed when this vacuum is filled."

—Pastor Narain Richard, Gospel Assembly Church, Elmont, New York

"After reading this book, it was not only refreshing, but it reinforced the need to guarantee the legacy of spiritual fatherhood from generation to generation as many fathers today are transitioning to be with the Lord. It is obvious the batons are passing, and the sons and daughters are becoming parents. Thus, without books like this one, we could lose the experiential insights, personal walks, and biblical extrapolation that is derived from the Word of God to guide us with proper parenting. This is a must read for every ministry, and the time has come to reignite the spirit of true fatherhood in the body of Christ to reassure a safe generation to follow."

—Bishop Eric D. Garnes, D.Min, MPS, Primate, Kingdom International Consortium

For foreign and subsidiary rights, contact the author.

Cover design: Sara Young

ISBN: 978-1-954089-34-1   1 2 3 4 5 6 7 8 9 10

Printed in the United States of America

WHERE HAVE ALL THE FATHERS GONE?

CREATING A LONG-LASTING LEGACY

DR. DAVID A LAZARUS

DREAM
RELEASER
ENTERPRISES

Dedication
On this year, my 40ᵗʰ in ministry, I dedicate this book to my wife, Neela. For your commitment, dedication, faithfulness to the call, and legacy you have helped me create, I thank you. I pray the spiritual sons and daughters who have been birthed through our ministry become destiny changers—not only for themselves but also for all they come in contact with. To my biological children, thank you for walking this journey with me and supporting me through the 40 years that we have been in ministry. Your sacrifices will be greatly rewarded.

Forewords

In an attempt to shed light on such an invaluable work Bishop David Lazarus has done in the writing of this book, he has captured the model that will sustain the legacy of those who spent their lives establishing a dream that would become their reality. The father/son relationship demonstrated in the pages of this book will set us back on track to building healthy kingdom families, ministries, and organizations. The restoration of families, communities, and great nations are found in these pages.

What Bishop Lazarus is proposing is more than a thought-provoking read; it's a formula that will heal the fear of trusting unfaithful men and women. What we will discover as we read is that sons and daughters are stimulated by the vision of a true father. God spoke promises to fathers that extend for generations, and only a father can teach a son or daughter the correct way to carry a promise from God.

Heaven has smiled on Bishop Lazarus for the content of this book and also favored him with a proven model of which I have been privileged to experience. I'm blessed to add my validation to a project in writing that will free our organizations from the orphan spirit. The answer to the inner pain from which all orphans will seek permanent relief is found in a father. 1 Corinthians 4:15 says, "For though ye have ten thousand instructors in Christ, yet have ye not many fathers: for in Christ Jesus I have begotten you through the gospel" (KJV). Most often these fathers are found in a Christ-led environment. Fathers with heavenly characteristics are rare, but they still exist. Not only will you experience Bishop David Lazarus' writing, but you will feel the love of a father in these pages.

—Apostle Bishop Stephen A. Davis

The most painful and difficult question I am asked by leaders worldwide is the topic of discussion in this book. In leadership roundtables with church and corporate leaders, there is open dialog with no subject off the table. It happens usually toward the conclusion of the day. Someone who has been absorbing a daylong leadership download will fidget for a minute, hesitate, raise their hand, and with some disclaimers, ask the same question I am asked repeatedly. The words are varied but the question is the same: *"What is your greatest regret in your leadership journey?"*

I remember in my earlier years, I gave a variety of answers trying to be congruent with the discussions and topics of that particular leadership roundtable. Those answers were not wrong and usually were found helpful by the leaders in the room.

However, when that question became a recurring theme regardless of the continent I was on, I gave it much more thought. When I arrived at my answer, I went into introspective mode. I began asking myself, "Why didn't I know this answer the first time I was asked this question years before now?"

I'm a fairly self-aware person and don't have challenges with being brutally honest, especially with myself. So why didn't I answer the question the first time?

Pain.

Deep pain from a place of huge deficit.

The ultimate answer to "What is your greatest regret in your leadership journey?" is that in my leadership journey, I did not have mentors, coaches, and covering fathers.

Just like my friend and author of this book, Bishop David Lazarus, I, too, was raised in a pastor's home. He, too, was not able to attend Bible college and was a self-taught man of God. I did go to Bible college and beyond. Yet, what I needed deep down was leadership, guidance, coaching, affirmation, correction, unconditional love, total acceptance, and to honor someone by serving them.

I have been blessed to be on this planet for almost seven decades. I was born and raised in a pastor's home, and I have graduated from institutions of higher learning. In short, I have been around leaders all my life. Yet to this day, I don't recall someone saying to me, "Sam, I see some gifts and talents in your life. Allow me to guide you so you don't make the same mistakes and help you not only accelerate your leadership journey but also lead a healthy life in every aspect of your being..."

Now, I have mentors and coaches who have helped me greatly through life's journey. They are my friends and confidants. They have permission to ask me difficult, probing questions. We do life together.

What I love about Bishop Lazarus' passionate heart and this book is you don't have to go through his pains, disappointment, and setbacks. You can learn and grow for yourself and others placed in your path.

Thank you, Bishop Lazarus, for pouring your life into this book so we can learn, grow, and help others.

—Sam Chand, Friend of David Lazarus

Contents

Introduction: My Motivation 13

Chapter 1. The Need for Spiritual Fathers 19

Chapter 2. Spiritual Covering 31

Chapter 3. Pitfalls for Spiritual Children 43

Chapter 4. Function of Fathers 55

Chapter 5. Spiritual Fathering 67

Chapter 6. Honoring Fatherhood 77

Chapter 7. The Blessing.................... 89

Chapter 8. Learning from the Master....... 105

Chapter 9. The Teachable Spirit 119

Chapter 10. Transfer to the Son............. 139

My Motivation

In the year 2020, I arrived at my 68th birthday. More importantly, the year also marked my 40th anniversary in ministry. Born and raised in a pastor's home, as I matured from a boy to a young man, I chose to live differently than many of my peers. I never backslid or ran into the world, and I never drank, smoked, or hung out with worldly friends. I made that decision because of what my father taught me and the faith that he demonstrated before my eyes. In addition, I saw the struggles and challenges he faced, which made me even more determined to live a righteous life. He was not able to attend Bible school and never had the benefits of a mentor or a coach. All that he knew was what he had taught himself.

My father launched his ministry in 1965 and built a successful congregation of approximately 300 people. In 1979, I sensed God calling me to follow in his steps and enter the ministry as well. By this time, I had completed my biblical studies and obtained a diploma from the Assemblies of God Church. Aside from my studies, everything I ever knew about God and church was instilled into my life by my father. He was my mentor, coach, and teacher. I became a full-time pastor in 1980, moving from Mount Edgecombe, a small community in KwaZulu-Natal, South Africa, to Benoni, located just east of Johannesburg—a trip of nearly seven hours. I was brought in by the church's superintendent to pastor a denominational church known as the Pentecostal Protestant Church.

I started pastoring that church on June 1, 1980 with six families in attendance. I soon found myself caught up in the same struggle as my father; I had no mentor, coach, or teacher. However, knowing God had called me, I decided to persevere and continue to run this race. Over the next few years, the church began to grow. As what usually happens, growth brought growing pains. Still lacking anyone to turn to, in 1985 I enrolled at Rhema Bible Training Centre in Johannesburg and furthered my studies and understanding of ministry. At the end of 1986, I received my diploma.

While attending Rhema, I made a few close friends, including friendships with a few lecturers. These men I surrounded myself with helped take my ministry to the next level. As I pastored the church, it grew, and a number of prominent people from other churches joined our congregation. Among those taking membership were some excellent musicians, singers, and teachers. Take note that I did not father these men and women; they joined me after being mentored or fathered already.

As the years went by, some of these men and women who joined to help me in ministry ultimately caused division and church splits, but I still persevered in ministry faithfully. I never learned from my mistakes because as other gifted, anointed, and talented people joined the church, I still brought them into leadership and used them to help me in ministry. I needed all the help I could get because I wanted to grow the ministry in numbers. I was number-conscious more than being church-health conscious. As the years went by, alas, it seemed like I was facing some kind of church split or division nearly every other year. I realized being humble and kind while helping other men or women whom I hadn't fathered as I tried to help unlock their destiny was not really helping the situation. Instead, they were trying to birth their own ministries, using my ministry as a platform.

Seeking Direction

In the year 2000, I started seeking the Lord intensely, asking for His direction and guidance to help eliminate this curse of church splits and division over my life and ministry. One day, I heard the Holy Spirit speaking distinctly, saying, "If you don't raise up your own spiritual sons and daughters and release them into ministry, you will have continuous problems with church splits." He told me I needed to handpick men and women from within the ministry who had been faithful, committed, and dedicated to God, the ministry, and our vision. It was these men and women whom I would father and raise up as spiritual sons and daughters. One profound thing the Spirit said the day He spoke to me was, "Inheritance and blessings are released to sons and daughters, not hirelings and wolves."

So, after much prayer and guidance by the Holy Spirit, I handpicked approximately 50 dedicated men and women in ministry and started a training program to raise up spiritual sons and daughters for ministry. To obtain knowledge, I studied the Scripture as it pertained to fathers and sons. I studied relationships like the one God had with His Son, Jesus, Adam in the garden, Abraham and Isaac, Jacob and his 12 sons, Moses and Joshua, Eli and Samuel, Elijah and Elisha, Jesus and His 12 disciples, Paul and Timothy, and others. In this program, I taught the trainees such subjects as covenant, covenant relationships, knowing the heart of the Father, the Father's DNA, vision, faithfulness, betrayal and blessings of a spiritual father, and servant leadership.

To date, the Lord has helped me raise spiritual sons within our ministry and many other parts of the world.

My wife and I have established 10 churches in South Africa and released spiritual sons and daughters to shepherd those flocks. These spiritual sons and daughters submit to me and carry the vision the Lord has bestowed in my heart for those local communities. They tithe to the local house regularly. These 10 churches work in unity, supporting and helping each other in every way. I also have spiritual sons and daughters in India, Zimbabwe, Swaziland, and Mauritius. Through this revelation and teaching, God helped me to preserve the church and protect it from church splits.

Over the years, I have seen young pastors who have never been fathered come out of Bible school orseminary, or lead churches. I have observed the pain they endure as they go through conflict and challenges from contentious members, other staff members, elders, or board members. I have seen so many experienced men and women of God trying to lead while they are bleeding. Many give up because of emotional breakdowns. Often, this is because they have not raised spiritual sons and daughters who can support them in ministry and help implement their vision. My spiritual sons and daughters and I have helped many along this journey of ministry. They can bear witness and testify about the blessings they have received through these teachings. They can allude to how having the covering of spiritual parents can help you avoid so many pitfalls and challenges in ministry. In having spiritual parents, you receive mentoring, guidance, and support as they provoke you into your destiny.

Challenges of Leadership

I don't share this to throw stones at any past associates in ministry but to point out this fact of life: In human relationships, there will always be friction and disagreements. Resolving them isn't always easy. Sometimes these problems cause separation as they did with Paul and John Mark. Successful leadership calls for close, supportive relationships to help the leader navigate these waters. Fathering sons and daughters is also necessary to prepare these children for the day they will take the father's place.

Men and women of God, if everything you have worked for, everything you have built, and everything you have established crumbles after your demise, then you will be a failure. There must be a continuity of your legacy. Your spiritual sons and daughters ought to be the carriers of your legacy. Men and women of God are to build God's kingdom, not a personal empire while preparing themselves for retirement. Build God's kingdom, and when spiritual sons or daughters receive the baton of continuity because they have been taught to serve, they will take care of you, honor you, and give you the assurance that your voice will be echoed in the generations to come.

To illustrate the value of this teaching, I served my spiritual father for 15 years before his demise. My spiritual father left me an inheritance, which is a beautiful property, buildings, and congregation, because I took care of him personally. Although he has departed from this earth, I still choose to take care of his wife, who is my spiritual mother. She, too, can teach on this subject, which is founded on God's Word. I trust this introduction will help you better understand why I felt compelled to write this book. I hope it also provides you with a deeper revelation of the crying need for more spiritual fathering in the worldwide church today.

CHAPTER ONE

The Need for Spiritual Fathers

I came from a generation of preachers who grew up in ministry without the benefits of spiritual fathers. In general, we live in a fatherless generation where far too many fathers are absent from families and homes. This is tragic because the spirit of fatherlessness that creates the wandering, aimless, and purposeless generation prevailing across the world is now being carried into our churches. Presently, the church lacks spiritual fathering and covering.

Like many others, I gathered knowledge about this teaching through books, audio recordings, seminars, and conferences. I have wondered how much more effective I would have become in ministry if someone had taken a personal interest in the call of God on my life. I believe Scripture indicates the necessity for spiritual fathers in our lives. As the church adheres more closely to the ideal of fatherhood and its apostolic calling, we can expect the hearts of spiritual fathers to be restored towards the sons and daughters of God and in the house of God.

Still, my experience shows the serious lack of spiritual fathers and how we as pastors need to act to restore this spirit to ministry. Spiritual fathers provide a safe environment to grow. The role of a spiritual father is to raise up spiritual children to nurture, protect, and pour out knowledge, understanding, wisdom, and counsel into their lives. His primary goal is to see his son or daughter grow in the knowledge and understanding of Jesus Christ and fulfil God's call upon their lives.

Fathers also train and prepare their sons and daughters for the transition from adolescence to adulthood. Everyone gets older chronologically, but not everyone matures. Spiritual fathers get their children to think about the vital nature of maturity as they place challenges on their children to grow. To promote growth, spiritual fathers inject a spirit of excellence into their sons and daughters. Placing such demands on the life of spiritual children is good because it helps them face—and overcome—personal challenges that can buffet their success and achievements. As children submit to their instructions, they will enter a new level of triumph.

Spiritual fathering and sonship is one of the most powerful truths in the Bible. It can be a source of blessing if done by the guidance of the Holy Spirit. (However, if done in the flesh, it can be one of the most damaging doctrines taught.) The terms "spiritual fathers" and "spiritual sons" are grounded in Scripture. In the Old Testament, the first book, Genesis, opens with Father and Son, and the final book, Malachi, closes with Father and Son. In the New Testament, the first chapter of the first book, Matthew, introduces us to Father and Son, and the last book, Revelation, ends with Father and Son.

Jesus Christ, the Perfect Example

Searching the Scripture about fathering will lead to Jesus as the best (indeed, the only perfect) example. As Hebrews 2:13 says of Him, "Here am I, and the children the Lord has given me" (NIV). Jesus called His 12 disciples, whom we know as His spiritual sons. Christ loved His 12 sons and cared about them very much.

Even though Peter, James, and John were close to Him in ministry, He did not have any favorites or discriminate in regard to the disciples' relationship with Him. This can be seen through His encounter with the mother of the sons of Zebedee in Matthew 20:20-28. She came to Jesus and said, "Grant that these two sons of mine may sit, one on Your right hand and the other on the left, in Your kingdom" (NKJV). Ultimately, He told her the issue was not for Him to decide, but His Father.

Jesus blessed His 12 sons at all times and met their every need. He imparted to them His wisdom, knowledge, and understanding. He taught them about His heavenly Father and reflected the Father's love and kindness through His life. When Phillip asked Jesus to show them the Father, He replied, "He who has seen Me has seen the Father" (John 14:9, NKJV).

This close affinity between Father and Son is one reason the prophecy that appears in Malachi is so powerful: "Behold, I will send you Elijah the prophet before the coming of the great and dreadful day of the Lord. And he will turn the hearts of the fathers to the children, and the hearts of the children to their fathers, lest I come and strike the earth with a curse" (Malachi 4:5-6, NKJV).

Here, Malachi was prophesying to the church that before the great and notable day of the Lord's return to this earth, God would release upon the earth *the spirit of Elijah*. One of the spirits that Elijah functioned in was the spirit of *fatherhood*, which will turn the heart of fathers to their sons and the hearts of sons to their fathers.

The Return of Fatherhood

Jesus invested much time with His sons to help them reach their full potential and become successful. He taught them about God and how to do ministry while training them, raising them up, and empowering them.

He gave them the authority to do ministry. In Luke 10, Jesus sent out His sons in groups of two to go and preach, teach, cast out devils, and heal the sick. In other words, He created a platform for them to do ministry.

When the sons came back from their assignment, they told Jesus, "Lord, even the demons are subject to us in Your name" (Luke 10:17, NKJV). Spiritual fathers set up platforms for their spiritual sons and daughters and introduce them to their friends and associates. When their sons or daughters walk in a greater anointing, he rejoices with them and does not get jealous, bitter, or envious. Spiritual fathers want to see their spiritual children walk and live in a greater anointing. Spiritual fathers are not threatened by the anointing and grace that flows through the lives of their spiritual offspring.

Jesus gave His spiritual sons access into His daily life; they did not have to go through a secretary to schedule any one-on-one time with Him. They had direct access to Him and received the opportunity to ask Him any questions dealing with ministry or their relationship with Him. They had an open-door relationship with Jesus, which built confidence into their lives and made ministry much easier for them.

Jesus believed in the ones whom no one else believed in. He took the ones who did not make the cut for formal rabbi training and transformed them into some of the greatest ministers in history. A true father believes in his sons and daughters and gets the best out of them. One of Jesus's focuses was to see God's destiny come to pass through His spiritual sons. Today, true fathers want to see a continuity of their legacy through their sons and daughters. Fathers do not give birth to spiritual sons for them (the children) to serve only the father; sons and daughters are legacy carriers and destiny builders. Fake fathers are interested solely in their own vision and ministries and thus only want sons and daughters to help them build the father's empire. Authentic spiritual fathers will teach their sons how to lead and become fathers themselves, or teach daughters to become mothers.

Father-Child Dynamic

Many of us were taught that Adam was the first creation of the human race, but the full story goes deeper than that. The end of the extended reverse genealogy in Luke 3:23-38 concludes by tracing Jesus back to the beginning as "the son of Enoch, the son of Seth, the son of Adam, the son of God" (Luke 3:38, NKJV). This shows us Adam was the created son of God, the birth of a supernatural Father and Son. (The divine God fathering humanity, Adam.) God expected the relationship that existed between God the Father and Jesus Christ at the time of creation and the relationship that existed between God the Father and Adam in the garden of Eden to have its continuity throughout creation. After the fall, humankind lost the grace of the supernatural fathering and covering of God. Throughout the generations, God sent prophets, judges, and priests, seeking to reconcile humans with God.

The Old Testament contains several sterling examples of fathering and sonship, such as Moses and Joshua, and Elijah and Elisha. They were imitating what began in Genesis, "Then God said, 'Let us make man in our image'" (Genesis 1:26, NKJV). Father speaking to Son said, "LET US make man in OUR image." This verse is further amplified in John 1:1-3 (NKJV): "In the beginning was the Word, and the Word was with God, and the Word was God. He was in the beginning with God. All things were made through Him, and without Him nothing was made that was made." John 1:1 teaches that Jesus Christ was from the beginning with God, while John 1:3 specifies everything that was made was made through Him.

This reveals the intimacy and oneness that existed between Father and Son. The Father and Son relationship existed from the beginning of creation. This is the same relationship that existed when God created Adam in His likeness and image. He breathed into Adam His breath of life, which is how Adam became a living soul. Appreciating the profound nature of this relationship can help us grasp Paul's emphasis on the importance of spiritual fathering: "For though you might have ten thousand instructors in Christ, yet you do not have many fathers; for in Christ Jesus I have begotten you through the gospel. Therefore I urge you, imitate me" (1 Corinthians 4:15-16, NKJV).

This is where Paul introduced the importance of spiritual fathering and sonship. We must take note Paul was not Timothy's biological father. Instead, Paul led Timothy to Jesus Christ and mentored him in his Christian faith. Paul then addressed Timothy as his son, something he also did with Onesimus (Philemon 1:10) and Titus (Titus 1:4).

Exposure to a spiritual father is one of the most refreshing and empowering relationships a person can enjoy. Spiritual fathers do not replace natural, biological fathers; therefore, we should not expect spiritual fathers to treat spiritual sons as natural-born children. In fact, spiritual fathers should not overstep the role of the natural father or attempt to be a biological father to their spiritual sons or daughters. If the natural father is present, a spiritual father should work hand-in-hand with the development of a son or daughter while respecting the biological father's role. Spiritual fathers must not get to a place where biological fathers become insecure about their relationship with their biological son or daughter.

Identifying Sons and Daughters

Not everyone who attends our ministry is a spiritual son or daughter. Some are autonomous sheep, disgruntled goats, or barbarous wolves. There are also good people who are, for various reasons, only passing through. This is likely a similar scenario in your church, no matter where in the world you live.

This reality raises the question: Do you know who your spiritual sons and daughters are? Apostolic grace is the grace of reproduction, multiplication of grace, and succession. The Holy Spirit revealed to me that sons and daughters in the ministry can be identified through two major characteristics:

1) By their spiritual pursuits

There are many who pray with a desire to receive what Elisha received, a *double portion* of the spirit; however, such double portions are an inheritance for sons and daughters. Elisha received a double portion because he pursued Elijah. In pursuing Elijah, Elisha served him and became his servant. Sons and daughters pursue their spiritual father. Many think Elisha pursued the prophet because Elisha sought his mantle, but 1 Kings 19:16 says that God told Elijah, "And Elisha the son of Shaphat of Abel Meholah you shall anoint as prophet in your place" (KJV). Elisha had no need to pursue Elijah because Elisha had already been anointed as a prophet.

Something in Elisha's heart beckoned him to pursue the old man. So he cooked his food, carried his water, washed his hands, waited on him, and served him. In 2 Kings 2, the Lord is preparing to take Elijah to heaven in a whirlwind: "Then Elijah said to Elisha, 'Stay here, please, for the Lord has sent me on to Bethel.' But Elisha said, 'As the Lord lives, and as your soul lives, I will not leave you!' So they went down to Bethel" (2 Kings 2:2, NKJV). This happens twice, when Elijah moves on to Jericho and then the Jordan. Each time, Elisha refuses to leave, pursuing Elijah to the other side of the Jordan, where he receives the mantle and a double portion of the spirit.

Children pursue their spiritual fathers. They have a hunger and a passion they will act on. In pursuit of growth, learning, and development, they position themselves to learn and grow in everything they do. One thing I have learned over the years is that you cannot teach passion; passion must be stirred up from within. I can read the Word, fast, and pray. I can motivate you and inspire you, but I cannot give you passion. Sons and daughters reveal themselves because they seek out fathers to learn from, and they are willing to do whatever it takes to get there. Pursuit tells you who someone really is.

2) They possess the father's DNA

Right after his remark about spiritual fathers, Paul tells the members of the Corinthian church, "Therefore I urge you, imitate me" (1 Corinthians 4:16, NKJV). Paul wants them to emulate his life and example because he is their spiritual father. Because sons and daughters possess the DNA of their father, they do not find it difficult to imitate him. Still, they must have a good perception of him. They need to know his passions, devotion, doctrine, servanthood, standards of integrity, and his love for the Word of God and family.

In short, the sons and daughters must have exposure to his apostolic grace so they can have a like-minded nature and can represent him in his absence. They reflect what Paul wrote to the church at Philippi: "But I trust in the Lord Jesus to send Timothy to you shortly. For I have no one likeminded who will sincerely care for your state. For all seek their own, not the things which are of Jesus Christ. But you know his proven character, that as a son with his father he served with me in the gospel" (Philippians 2:19-22, NKJV). In verse 20, the Greek root of "like-minded" is *isopsuchos*, which means to have the same mind or spirit, equal in soul. Basically, this means the sons or daughters have a mindset identical to the father's. This like-minded nature is a crucial quality; not all sons or daughters can live up to this standard. Sons and daughters have the same sincere love and care for the body as the father. They will not exploit or divide the body or bring division to the body in his absence. Sons and daughters are well-acquainted with the father's preferences, down to the smallest details. They can actually tell you how the father feels, how he thinks, and his daily habits. Sons and daughters don't uncover the father's weaknesses to others. They cover and protect the grace and anointing over his life at all times.

Nor do sons or daughters exploit the father. They don't look out for benefits they can gain from exposure to him. They are not opportunistic or selfishly ambitious. Spiritual children point all things towards the father; they always want him to be seen or heard before they expose their own talents and giftings.

Sons and daughters are not doubled-tongued either. They know how to keep a secret whenever they are present with him. Maintaining confidentiality is one of the main characteristics of a true son or daughter. They are fully aware of their father's culture, doctrine, and beliefs. Sons and daughters stay in the father's house without causing division or dissension. They don't belong to or create any cliques in the body. Sons and daughters are loyal, faithful, dependable, trustworthy, and obedient. Whatever they do is from their heart as unto the Lord.

Spiritual Fathering

It is necessary for every born-again child of God to have spiritual parents. To understand spiritual truths and to get you to your spiritual destiny, you need to have spiritual parents in your life. King Saul asked David a question: 'Whose son are you?' (1 Samuel 17:58, NKJV). The book of Matthew starts with the genealogy of Jesus Christ, meaning everybody needs to have a genealogy. We are birthed from the seed of a natural father; all of us are born again by the Word of God but also through the influence of a man or woman of God.

Spiritual Parents

Spiritual parents are the person or persons who either brought you to salvation or the knowledge of your calling. They have been with you since the early stages of your walk with Christ. They were among the first to recognise your spiritual identity as well as your flaws and strengths. They help you as you begin your spiritual journey. They make the initial impartation of wisdom, order, knowledge, and understanding in your life. Only fools do not submit to higher spiritual authority.

Even though your connection to your spiritual parents may be a lifetime connection, this does not mean you will stay under their ministry forever as you complete your spiritual growth. Still, it's important to maintain a certain level of accountability to your spiritual parents as you move out. Like a natural parent, they maintain a watchful eye on you from a distance, and always remain available should you need that fatherly or motherly shoulder. If you are not fathered well, over time you will run off the rails.

As spiritual children, you should not compromise your assignment, but learn who you are supposed to be with and stay there until God moves you. When choosing or accepting your spiritual parents, it is vital to take note of their character, spiritual covering, ministerial associations, and their spiritual children. There are four keys to remember about your spiritual parents:

1) They carry keys to your future and aren't in competition with you.
2) They help you break the cycle of degeneration.
3) They are appointed by God to help you in your spiritual journey and to bring out God's best in you.

4) They are crucial. One father (or mother) will do more than 10,000 motivational speakers.

Blessings Spiritual Fathers Provide

- True spiritual fathers have first learned to be sons themselves. This is a stage that cannot be skipped, although many attempt to father without processing sonship in their own lives. This is what separates true spiritual fathers from the rest. They have learned to walk as a son before their Father in heaven and before their spiritual father on earth. Sons who resist fathering or who have never been fathered should never become spiritual fathers to any young man or woman in ministry. If you have not been fathered, you will not know the biblical principles of how to father young children.

- They provide a safe environment of life and protection. The foundation of any father-and-son (or daughter) relationship must be built on adding value, love, care, protection, and acceptance. Relationships with spiritual fathers and spiritual children should not be forced or include any obligations or preconditions. Spiritual fathers provide an environment of love and care because love is their highest value. In an atmosphere of love and acceptance, spiritual sons and daughters feel loved and protected. It is easy for them to break through limitations and grow in their calling. When you are around true spiritual fathers, you feel encouraged, strengthened, and ready to take on the world. Connecting to a spiritual father is based on relationship, not on joining an organization. True spiritual fathers don't lord it over their children, nor do they act as dictators; they love, care, nurture, and serve in order to be served. A healthy relationship between father and child brings mutual honor and respect.

- They share personal integrity and authentic experiences with God. Paul was an example of this to Timothy when he reminded him, "But you have carefully followed my doctrine, manner of life, purpose, faith, longsuffering, love, perseverance, persecutions, afflictions" (2 Timothy 3:10-11, NKJV). Spiritual fathers do not appear overnight because it takes years of their own seasoning to establish firm integrity and authentic life transformation in their own walk.

Almost all genuine spiritual fathers have been through some intense sifting and testing of their faith. They have learned to fight the good fight of faith and emerged strong and victorious. Spiritual fathers set good examples through their own lives. They just don't teach; their lives are a message because they have been through fire and high water. Many have been through financial troubles, health issues, contentious relationships, or challenges with rebellious or wayward children.

In learning from their experiences, they can be encouraging, empowering, and godly spiritual fathers. Their lives provide a model for us, which is one of the best ways to learn. Sitting in a classroom or reading a book can provide some knowledge or resources, but it cannot compare to or teach the modeling that a spiritual father brings to the table. Watching how role models live their lives, share their love, react to challenges, forgive when hurt, deal with emotional pain, manage their money and family, treat their spouses, and relate to their children is the best way to engage the learning and growth process. This is a prime reason we need more of them—to help the church's sons and daughters mature in faith.

CHAPTER TWO

Spiritual Covering

Many ministries and organizations don't believe in spiritual covering (from humans) because they say it is not biblical. Manuel Pascoal, the pastor of Siloam Word of Truth in Edenvale, South Africa, thinks otherwise. "I have come to believe in spiritual fatherhood through the revelation of the Word of God," says Manuel, whose early struggles in ministry mirrored mine. "To me, it is more than a theory or concept, but a life experience. It is the way of life in the kingdom of God."

Raised in a rural farming community, at the age of 19, Manuel decided to follow Jesus as his Savior. After experiencing a radical spiritual transformation, he sensed God's call to ministry and diligently pursued God's will. Connecting to a vibrant ministry, he served and grew. Eight years later, the Lord opened the door for him to attend Bible school, about the same time he married his beautiful wife, Fiona. As they grew in the Word of God and ministry, they also received more responsibilities and ministry experience. However, he also faced many challenges, pressures, disappointments, and misunderstandings.

As much as he loved God and His work, Manuel soon realized he needed help. Fiona had experienced spiritual fatherhood while growing up and advised him he needed that in his life as well. At the time, he didn't know much about spiritual fatherhood, had received little teaching on the subject, and had no experience of it in his current ministry. Not surprisingly, at that point he also found himself broken, wounded, and lonely. Discouragement set in, and he felt like a failure in God's work—until God led him to our ministry and came under my care and that of my wife, Mama Neela Lazarus.

"I noticed Bishop Lazarus did ministry quite differently," Manuel wrote in a reflection about his experiences. "He was humble, courteous, caring, and had a fatherly grace upon his life. He was genuinely concerned about others. He wanted others to grow and showed love as if they were his own children. His kindness drew me to hope again. I started learning about spiritual fatherhood and sonship. This changed my life and ministry completely, including my entire motivation and perspective for ministry."

Among the many lessons Manuel learned were:
- The functions of sons and daughters in God's kingdom
- Obeying your parents in the Lord
- God's house as a family
- Knowing the Father's heart

Manuel explains that being a spiritual father and mother is more than just being a counselor, a mentor, or even a coach. It's about the spiritual grace given by God, which includes deep love and care. This creates a heart-felt reality, birthing a covenant love and relationship that forges unbreakable bonds. He says this willingness to share life and give freely of one's time and trust provides a spiritual covering and oversight that unlocks God-given potential and destiny. Manuel says:

We see this in the Bible between God the Father and Jesus the Son. We are intrigued by this wonder in the life and ministry of Elijah and Elisha that yielded a double portion. Undoubtedly, we witness this in the life of the prophet, Moses, and Joshua, the son of Nun. This relationship is also seen in the New Testament and shines brightly in the life and ministry of the apostle Paul and Timothy.

We are forever grateful to God for His grace to have us under the care of a spiritual father and spiritual mother. We feel loved, cared for, equipped, and well-covered spiritually. Bishop Lazarus released us into ministry, which he founded in Edenvale (Johannesburg). Both Fiona and I are pastoring this beautiful church. Spiritual covering has helped lift the burdens of ministry so that we can serve and help God's people with such great freedom.

People Matter

Adrian Jacobs, pastor of Siloam Word of Truth in Brakpan, South Africa, says the biggest lesson he learned from serving alongside me is that people matter. Ministers of the gospel must have a heart for people and accept, love, and receive God's people as their own. Adrian says:

This lesson refreshes itself in every season of life and deepens the commitment he feels towards God's people and His house. From this lesson came the single greatest gem of wisdom for all ministers: Lead God's people according to His will and not the whims of the people—pastors don't want to be like Moses and miss their promised land.

Life changed drastically for my family and I in 2015 when Bishop Lazarus installed me as the lead pastor of the campus he birthed and led for many years. This was a pivotal moment of transition and change, but again he showed his leadership ethic and principles. He stood head and shoulders above many in ministry. My family and I lead a dynamic church and ministry because my spiritual father and mother took us and said that we were not servants but sons and daughters. They restored us to the purpose and plan of God for our lives.

Making a Difference

I hope these words don't strike you as self-serving. I included them as examples of authentic testimonies about the difference a spiritual father (and mother) can make in one's life, just as it did in mine. I believe implementing this concept can change the destiny of numerous pastors' and church members' lives across the world. The oversight of a spiritual father is not only biblical but crucial in the lives of sons and daughters and leaders. In saying that, I should caution that spiritual fathers should never lord over, dictate, control, or manipulate their spiritual offspring or whomever else they lead. Yet, oversight is necessary in the areas of decision-making, advice, moral failure, or other crises.

For Renal Mannikam, pastor of Siloam Word of Truth in Sandton, a part of metropolitan Johannesburg, serving for more than a decade as my administrative assistant gave him an up-close and personal look at ministers who drew close to me in a time of brokenness or weariness. They sought a counselor and an experienced, seasoned minister who could help them heal and find their own path in their calling. They found more than that as many began to realize my care and compassion extended beyond lessons of lecturers or religious seniors they had encountered previously. My compassion for them was not just as a minister, but as a husband, father, and someone with personal concern for their well being. Renal says:

For a long time, it was the pain I witnessed in the lives of these blessed ministers that made me second-guess serving in a lead role in ministry. Bishop, however, often made mention of this and saw a possibility that I would rather have run away from. I suppose it was this part of my journey that today gives me a very soft spot for those who choose to commit to the work of the ministry.

There were also friends of Bishop Lazarus from across the globe who made indelible impressions on me as a growing minister. Whether locally, from the African continent, or the East or West, there were lessons learned because my relationship with Bishop granted me access to their various ministries. My own style and approach to ministry was found through some of these relationships that I was given the opportunity to experience.

One reason he appreciates having a spiritual father is not only how these experiences enriched his life journey, but because I saw more in him than he could see in himself. Lest you think I'm offering an overly rosy picture, Renal notes that our time together has not always been easy. We have shared sad days as well as happy ones, and disagreements as well as joy and much laughter. We have shared pulpits, traveled, and prayed together. Through our many seasons, Renal treasures me calling him his son as well as inviting him to serve in ministry while I offered mentorship, counsel, and discipline.

Key Lessons

Renal outlines the key ministry lessons he learned while working with me as:

1) Ministry is about people. No people equals no ministry. Therefore, care for the people.
2) Preach on purpose and you will not be wrong. There is always someone in the room seeking God for direction.
3) Visionary faith. He says he has yet to experience a fraction of what I have achieved in his ministry by simply trusting God. Yet even though this is a

lesson he doesn't expect will ever be mastered, it is an aspect of the vision he is constantly developing.

4) Care for those who work in ministry. The call of God should not limit the resources God has made available for those who work in ministry.

In addition, after a decade of administrative experience in ministry, the Lord opened the door for Renal to explore a course in the field of business and run a company that sold cleaning chemicals. This was previously unexplored territory for him. Although he later left business to enter full-time ministry, what helped him chart this new course were the lessons he had learned in the years of serving in ministry, observing my leadership, and gleaning insights on vision, excellence, and people. That helped him work with those around him and grow this "non-religious" marketplace endeavour.

"Clearly the expanse of Bishop's impact upon my life was beyond the four walls of the church," Renal says. "The writings of Paul in 1 Corinthians 4:15 ring true of the man who has guided me in my pursuit of destiny: 'For though you might have ten thousand instructors in Christ, yet you do not have many fathers; for in Christ Jesus I have begotten you through the gospel.' Bishop Lazarus has certainly encapsulated the role of a father, in my life and the many who have encountered his caring and compassionate character."

This relationship illustrates the truth that since spiritual covering and spiritual insight is relational, transparency is of utmost importance. All sons and daughters go through trying times and challenges. Therefore, they need to go to someone to consult and receive counsel, advice, encouragement, and sometimes correction so they can continue to pursue God's call on their lives.

Even if a senior pastor or leader does not fall into sin, there could be a challenge between him (or her) and the board of elders, a dispute with the local body, or other problems. At this point, a spiritual father or other spiritual covering can step in to become a mediator to resolve the issue.

This demonstrates another benefit of spiritual fathers: They enhance the way we think. A fathering presence helps improve our 'grid' and stretch us to see the bigger picture. Their teaching, counsel, wisdom, advice, and discipline opens us up to more wisdom than decades of research and acquiring knowledge can offer. It's amazing to see how spiritual fathers have become good thinkers. They never lack ideas that can build an organization.

Bring Children to Maturity

Spiritual fathers have great ambitions and desires for their spiritual sons and daughters. They want to see their children grow and mature into the full stature of their design. Many sons never grow up to become mature spiritual men, remaining stuck in adolescence because they were not fathered into the various stages of maturity necessary for growth. Paul says, "When I was a child, I spoke as a child, I understood as a child, I thought as a child; but when I became a man, I put away childish things" (1 Corinthians 13:11, NKJV).

In Acts 22:3, Paul talked about being schooled by Gamaliel, a Pharisee and noted expert in Mosaic Law. Since he was fathered and schooled in different areas of growth and maturity, Paul was well-equipped to later help his spiritual sons grow. Maturity is vital in your spiritual life; spiritual fathers will put demands on children to grow. Such demands are good, since they help sons and daughters face personal challenges that can buffet their efforts at achievement and success. As children submit to the instructions of a spiritual father in these areas, they will experience new levels of triumph. They can expect a spiritual father to motivate them to set goals and achieve them.

Release an Impartation

Impartation can often be misunderstood, but it is one of the greatest effects a father has on his sons and daughters. Children most of the time imitate their spiritual fathers. Among the Scriptures that address this:

- 2 Timothy 1:6: "Therefore I remind you to stir up the gift of God which is in you by the laying on of my hands" (KJV).
- 1 Thessalonians 2:8: "So, affectionately longing for you, we were well pleased to impart to you not only the gospel of God, but also our own lives, because you had become dear to us" (KJV).
- Romans 1:11-12: "For I long to see you, that I may impart to you some spiritual gift, so that you may be established—that is, that I may be encouraged together with you by the mutual faith both of you and me" (KJV).

Offer Accountability and Correction

While we are first accountable to God because He is our Judge, we are also accountable to the people God has placed over our lives. As Hebrews 13:17 instructs, "Obey those who rule over you and be submissive, for they watch over your souls as those who must give account. Let them do so with joy and not with grief, for that would be unprofitable for you" (KJV).

The words of this verse are quite significant. Those who watch over our souls will someday give an account of our lives to God. As leaders, they are placed by God as shepherds to watch over us. Because spiritual fathers must give an account of our souls to God, they should not be afraid to correct spiritual sons and daughters when they falter, fail, or do wrong. True spiritual fathers do not ignore wrongdoing or compromise with sin; they apply the rod of discipline so they can drive mischief far from their children's hearts. When discipline or correction is applied, true spiritual sons and daughters do not become arrogant or walk in rebellion or stubbornness. They walk in love because they want to grow and mature in their calling. Correction is designed to help sons and daughters grow spiritually and emotionally; mature children know how to handle correction. When spiritual fathers and spiritual sons or daughters have a healthy relationship, correction and discipline is a delight.

Release an Inheritance

Before addressing the subject of inheritance, I need to point out this truth: The giants that spiritual fathers fail to conquer will be the same giants their spiritual sons and daughters will face. For sons and daughters to enjoy a rich spiritual inheritance, they must stand beside their spiritual fathers and help them slay the giants the fathers face in their season. Remember, children do nothing to earn a spiritual inheritance from their spiritual fathers; it is a grace gift added to their journey.

A spiritual inheritance given to sons and daughters by their spiritual father gives them the grace to go even further than the father went. The delight and joy of every spiritual father is to see his children enjoy more success and see them go further than he did. His desire is to see them flow in a greater anointing and conviction and see them become better and greater articulators of the Word and visionaries of their destiny.

Other Benefits

- **They nurture.** Spiritual fathers help develop, take care of, protect someone or something, support, encourage, train, and educate those they are leading.
- **They shape and mould.** Spiritual fathers further the character of spiritual sons and daughters.
- **They instil purpose and unlock potential.** Spiritual fathers closely guide their spiritual sons and daughters in their journey to help them unlock their God-given potential and reach their destiny.

Instil Moral Values

Children are a biological parent's most valuable asset. It is every parent's dream to shape their children into responsible, amazing people. Besides giving them a good education, imparting moral values to their offspring is extremely important. Spiritual fathers need to do the same with their spiritual sons and daughters.

Imparting moral values such as honesty, self-discipline, patience, kindness, gratitude, forgiveness, respect, courtesy, servanthood, and personal responsibility are extremely important. The best way for a spiritual father to impart and teach moral values to his spiritual children is by being a good role model. No matter how old our spiritual sons or daughters or how well they can teach or preach, an element of carnality is found in almost all of us. To instil moral values, it is important to break this element of carnality.

Other moral values that are extremely important are:

- Love: teaching them to be generous with their affection towards others
- Determination: encouraging them to take on challenges and be confident

- Consideration: teaching them to think about the feelings of others
- Correction: helping them receive discipline without rebellion

This final point is illustrated by Hebrews 12:5-8: "And you have forgotten the exhortation which speaks to you as to sons: 'My son, do not despise the chastening of the Lord, nor be discouraged when you are rebuked by Him; for whom the Lord loves He chastens, and scourges every son whom He receives.' If you endure chastening, God deals with you as with sons; for what son is there whom a father does not chasten? But if you are without chastening, of which all have become partakers, then you are illegitimate and not sons" (KJV).

Human nature is prideful, stubborn, and rebellious. The spiritual nature given to Christ's followers is meek, submissive, loving, and seeking an intimate relationship with the heavenly Father. Spiritual fathers can help lead us to that which the heart truly desires; therefore, an open and transparent relationship is important.

CHAPTER THREE

Pitfalls for Spiritual Children

Thus far, I have addressed the blessings and benefits offered by spiritual fathers. As part of this discussion, I need to point out the twin pitfalls that spiritual sons and daughters need to guard against: familiarity and presumption.

Developing close relationships is hard work, but it is fundamental in apostolic ministry. While training their sons or daughters, some spiritual fathers have displayed their weakness and humanity, only to discover that some children are not able to handle such transparency. As the old saying goes, familiarity can breed contempt—but contempt is a disrespectful behavior that leads to presumptuous actions. Jesus could not do powerful ministry work in His hometown of Nazareth because many thought of Him as nothing more than a carpenter's son: "So they were offended at Him. But Jesus said unto them, 'A prophet is not without honor except in his own country and in his own house.' Now He did not do many mighty works there because of their unbelief" (Matthew 13:56-58, NKJV).

Because of their familiarity with Him as Joseph's son, the Nazarites did not accept the ministry of Jesus and deprived themselves of seeing Him perform any mighty works. The same thing can happen to sons and daughters who act contemptuously toward their spiritual fathers.

The Need for Fathers

We live in an era where people are manifesting a lack of fathering in their lives. Far too many people have never had a normal relationship with their biological fathers and thus haven't received a father's blessing or affirmation while growing up. The drive for a father's approval is so great that some respond to this fatherlessness by engaging in self-destructive, addictive behaviours. Some have become workaholics in a desperate attempt to accomplish great things and somehow fill the vacuum left in their hearts. I believe God has raised up the church as a family to provide spiritual fathers and mothers who can become surrogate parents, helping to heal the pain of rejection in the hearts of these spiritual children.

Though I quoted the verse in the first chapter, 1 Corinthians 4:15 merits repeating here: "For though you might have ten thousand instructors in Christ, yet you do not have many fathers" (KJV). In the church today, we have many teachers, instructors, and mentors, but we don't have many fathers. Spiritual fathers are hard to find. Therefore, it is imperative for pastors and leaders to go beyond their professional titles and become relationally involved as spiritual parents with the people under their pastoral care.

With the incredible breakdown in families, the church is now the only hope to restore the vacuum left in the hearts of a fatherless society. I have noticed there are too many men and women who refuse to allow spiritual fathers the emotional access necessary to nurture them. Correcting this will require great depth of understanding, patience, and compassion, but it is the kind of vital task that will show the love of Christ where nothing else can succeed.

Reasons for Rejection

Many men and women reject spiritual fathers because their wounded fatherhood image means they no longer trust male authority figures. When children or young men experience abandonment from their biological fathers—be that physical or emotional—it leaves permanent, emotional scars that can only be healed by God through forgiveness, our heavenly Father's love and acceptance, and by receiving a spiritual father into one's life. Men who were abandoned by their biological father grow up not trusting male figures and tend to gravitate towards female authority, even to the point of receiving spiritual mothers while not trusting spiritual fathers.

Refusing Accountability

Accountability is a vital ingredient in every person's life. When you hold people accountable for their actions, you are effectively teaching them to value their work and relationships (especially with the one to whom they are accountable). Accountability increases confidence and trust and brings out transparency in a relationship. Many men who profess a desire for spiritual fathering don't like accountability because of the manner in which they grew up—independently, not having to be accountable to a parent, elder, or other leader. Growing up without a mentor creates major challenges in one's life. Spiritual seekers who have never had biological fathers involved in their lives often find it difficult to have someone watch over or correct them.

Fear of Disappointment

A father's affirmation with biological or spiritual children is the most powerful experience a child—especially a male—can ever have. Spiritual fathers need to understand that when a young man or boy opens their heart, soul, and emotions to them, they need to be gentle, kind, and tolerant because of where they come from. That may be a place of rejection, abuse, abandonment, hurt, pain, or all the above. Now they are looking for spiritual parents who can love, protect, and listen to them. They crave spiritual parents whom they can trust and will not walk away from them.

Spiritual fathers need to understand the incredible power behind their words and actions. Any words they speak or actions they take that degrades their spiritual child's ability, value, or self-worth can emotionally devastate and destroy them. Spiritual sons and daughters live in fear of being rejected again by another in whom they entrust their heart. Appraisals do much good for spiritual sons or daughters who have gone through emotional pain and stress; it energizes their self-worth and confidence. Spiritual children must always be loved unconditionally, not for what they can do or when they are at their best. Fatherless men and women produce fatherless sons and daughters in the Lord.

Victims of Abuse

Men and women who have suffered verbal or physical abuse by their biological fathers tend to mistrust spiritual fathers and spiritual authority. Our brains are trained to make associations with other pain or pleasure based on how we were raised. An abused son or daughter will often associate all father figures (whether good or bad) with pain and abuse. Thus, they tend to shy away from spiritual fathering until they are healed or able to trust again. At times, many sons and daughters have experienced great pain in church when spiritual fathers have used them for their own advantage.

Exposure to Weakness

Sons and daughters must realize when serving a man of God that this man has weaknesses, including the potential to fail and sin. Being overconfident in another human being and placing great faith and trust in that person can prove even more disappointing when a spiritual father gets caught up in sin.

This is always a reality. Romans 3:23 says, "For all have sinned and fall short of the glory of God" (KJV). There is no perfect human aside from Jesus Christ. Therefore, spiritual fathers must learn to walk circumspectly and keep their respect before spiritual sons and daughters so they do not become discouraged, backslide, or even quit ministry when they are exposed to a father's sins or weaknesses. When anyone places a spiritual father on a pedestal, they are setting themselves up for trouble and a fall. Sin is found in all of us because of our forefather, Adam.

Lacking *The* Father's Love

Men who have not experienced the love of God or are not secure in God's love will never be anchored enough emotionally and spiritually to be secure in any other relationship. Only to the extent that we experience the love, security, and affirmation of the love of God as our Father will we be able to mimic that relationship. That is true whether it is with our biological father, spiritual father, or even as a father to our own children.

Lack of Authenticity

We live in a generation where there is little spiritual fathering. So many pastors and leaders are rising in many churches and denominations—writing books, producing podcasts and popular TV or internet programs, and generating social media followings—that many see pastoring as more of a job function than a divine calling. As a result, many pastors don't know how to function as a spiritual father. We cannot father someone if we have not been fathered, and we cannot father if we have not gone through the process of being a father. If we have not had the example of a good role model, we cannot model fatherhood.

Today churches are giving birth to spiritual children, but we do not have enough fathers who can break the curse of the orphan spirit over their lives and bring them to a place of love, care, and security. Spiritual sons and daughters will reject spiritual fathers if they ultimately discover the relationship is not authentic. For a true relationship to be birthed between spiritual children and spiritual fathers, there must be development in the following areas:

- Spiritual sons or daughters must have access into the life of their spiritual father.
- There must be personal interaction.
- When needed, children must receive regular input from their spiritual father.
- There must be accountability, conviction, affirmation, partnership in ministry, and even friendship.

Spiritual fathers must stay in constant contact and fellowship with their spiritual sons or daughters. The absence of biological fathers in homes has caused a serious decline in marriage and family as well as fragmentation of families. The church must take the lead in developing a community model of family and spiritual parenting that the world can latch onto. When spiritual fathers arise in our churches and give spiritual covering to hurting sons and daughters, there will be healing in those children's lives. Once healed from their brokenness and restored to the love of God the Father, they in turn will produce godly families, leading as godly fathers and mothers and breaking the curse of the orphan. Our world needs to see the church take the lead in family life as the church produces godly parents, but especially fathers.

The Orphan Spirit

Ever since Adam and Eve's sin alienated the human race from God the Father in the Garden of Eden, an orphan spirit has permeated the earth, causing untold damage. (By orphan, I am referring to a sense of abandonment, loneliness, alienation, and isolation.) After the fall in Eden, the fruit of the fleshly spirit resulted in jealousy, culminating in Cain murdering his brother Abel because God the Father didn't receive Cain's offering.

To make matters worse, in contemporary society, large amounts of people are not just alienated from God; they are brought up without the loving care and security of their biological fathers. Orphaned men have a hard time committing to their spouses, children, those in spiritual authority, and supervisors at work. They even have a hard time accepting and loving themselves. There are millions of incarcerated men who are acting out lives of violence and rebellion because their earthly fathers abandoned them.

The only way to break this orphan spirit is for people to be filled with a sense of the Father's love for them in Christ. This is what will enable them to become mature sons who serve God out of knowledge of His undeserved grace instead of trying to earn the Father's love through performance. The orphan spirit is perhaps the greatest curse on the earth today. It will take spiritual parents with great spiritual depth and authority to break and reverse this curse and in its place perpetuate a generational blessing.

Only when a person is healed of fatherlessness through the love of God can the orphan spirit become broken, and they can begin the process of entering mature sonship or daughtership. Sonship is so important that all of creation is presently crying out for the manifestation of the mature sons of God. An orphan has no mother or father. An orphan spirit can afflict Christians and non-Christians alike. It is insidious and no respecter of persons. Those who carry this spirit usually suffer from rejection and are always angry and moody.

The orphan spirit drives a person to feel like they always have to work hard to receive approval and acceptance from others. They have a performance-driven orientation, which makes them compete with others for recognition and survival. They are sensitive and defensive, always seeking the love they never received from their fathers or parents. Those who carry this spirit lead very complicated lives, with all the baggage they carry from their past, including their pain and hurts. Since many have not yet found themselves, they are always searching for their identity through their efforts. In extreme cases, they can be suicidal, bitter, angry, violent, and aggressive.

This spirit is a curse and needs to be broken, cancelled, and eradicated from our lives. Although people can be born again, saved, and faithfully attend church, many still live with an orphan mentality, the spirit of never quite measuring up or feeling "good enough." When people fail to deal with this kind of mentality, it can cause serious problems and challenges while people are growing up and even into their teenage and adult years. This will affect their personal relationships, marriage, and children.

Jesus Was NO Orphan

At His baptism, Jesus received a public affirmation from his Father: "This is My beloved Son. Hear Him!" (Luke 9:35, NKJV). This teaches us that Jesus had a Father and came from a Father. Jesus knew who He was, whose He was, and that He was the Father's beloved Son. Having affirmation from their father and the release of a fatherly blessing on their life before starting their mission is one of the greatest blessings a son or daughter can receive. Jesus's affirmation as a Son was not done privately but with a public endorsement on the day of His baptism. This affirmation in public gave Jesus the spirit of boldness, courage, and confidence. He knew His mission on earth came with the full support of the Father in heaven. He was not here on earth doing His will but the will of the Father. Armed and equipped with this knowledge, Jesus was ready to enter the desert and face the darkness and emerge victorious, conquering Satan.

Fatherless Generation

In Chapter 1, I mentioned Malachi 4:5-6 and God turning the hearts of fathers to the children, and the hearts of the children to their fathers. This is crucial to the future of our world. Better dads will produce better sons and daughters. We live in a fatherless generation; fatherlessness is one of the prevailing issues of our sin-sick world. Whether it is a father who is physically absent or one who is emotionally distant, the lack of fathers has left a noticeable mark on our society. To break the spirit of fatherlessness, men in particular need to be equipped to become better dads; men need to be more engaged in the lives of their children.

Nearly every problem in cultures across the globe can be directly or indirectly traced to fatherlessness in one form or the other. Children from fatherless homes are five times as likely to be poor than those from two-parent homes, 10 times more likely to be extremely poor, and twice as likely to be high school dropouts. Girls are three times more likely to become unwed mothers in their teens. From fatherless homes come 90 percent of runaways, 75 percent of suicides, and 70 percent of male prison inmates. When children have been brought up in broken homes or fatherless environments, boys in particular tend to model that behaviour (sometimes unconsciously). We emulate what we have observed in our homes while growing up.

Sonship by Adoption

The theme of adoption is woven throughout Scripture, serving to not only strengthen our Christian faith but to also encourage us as we press into the needs of waiting children. Sonship is the relationship between father and son (or daughter). Earlier, I mentioned Paul's emphasis on fatherhood in 1 Corinthians 4:15) This is essential to spiritual growth, since through the preaching and teaching of the Word by our spiritual fathers we experience transformation.

It is through this kind of life change, after we make the decision to follow Jesus as Lord and Savior, that we are adopted into God's family. This is verified by Romans 8:15-17, which says, "For you did not receive the spirit of bondage again to fear, but you received the Spirit of adoption by whom we cry out, 'Abba, Father.' The Spirit Himself bears witness with our spirit that we are children of God, and if children, then heirs—heirs of God and joint heirs with Christ, if indeed we suffer with Him, that we may also be glorified together" (KJV). Paul addressed this topic again in Galatians 4:4-6: "But when the fullness of the time had come, God sent forth His Son, born of a woman, born under the law, to redeem those who were under the law, that we might receive the adoption as sons. And because you are sons, God has sent forth the Spirit of His Son into your hearts, crying out, 'Abba, Father!'" (KJV).

This spirit of adoption is key to grasping our place in God's kingdom. In his letters, Paul talks about two spirits: a spirit of slavery—meaning you are bound to the world's laws, customs, and dictates, not as human chattel of another person—and the spirit of adoption. The spirit of slavery makes you a slave to the flesh and all its lusts and cravings, while the spirit of adoption makes you a child of God. To become a son or daughter of God, there is no need for physical intimacy or touch. We are made His spiritual children through the spirit of adoption.

Ephesians 1:4-6 offers this assurance: "He chose us in Him before the foundation of the world, that we should be holy and without blame before Him in love, having predestined us to adoption as sons by Jesus Christ to Himself, according to the good pleasure of His will, to the praise of the glory of His grace, by which He made us accepted in the Beloved" (KJV). When God adopts US into his family as sons and daughters, he breaks off the orphan spirit and brings us into a new social standing with Him.

God adopts us not because we are unworthy, but because we are worthy. As the children of God (by the Spirit), we have all the blessing and privileges that Jesus Christ has. Yet many children of God do not understand the unlimited resources of God that are at their disposal and thus live as orphans. Even in the natural, spiritual sons and daughters may not be connected to their spiritual fathers biologically or by blood, yet they are children of the family by the adoption of the Holy Spirit. Such rich, full blessings should never be ignored or taken for granted. By them we are rich, no matter what the size of our houses or bank accounts!

CHAPTER FOUR

Function of Fathers

The spirit of fatherlessness exhibits itself in a number of ways in today's church, but none are more glaring than the lack of respect many display for the spiritual fathers God has placed over them. During Old Testament days, most believers had no revelation of the value of prophets and servants of God, as seen by the numerous prophets who were martyred, persecuted, and thrown into prison. Even in present day, many men and women of God are ill-treated, have evil spoken about them, and face judgment and persecution.

Many general congregation members have no respect or honor for the local church pastor. From my regular visits to the U.S. and discussions with pastors there, I think this is as true in America as it is in South Africa (and other nations). Such disrespect often extends to evangelists, prophets, teachers, or other overseers, which tacitly ignores the gift such people represent to the church. Ephesians 4:11-12 tells us, "And He Himself gave some to be apostles, some prophets, some evangelists, and some pastors and teachers, for the equipping of the saints for the work of ministry, for the edifying of the body of Christ" (KJV).

My prayer is that the Holy Spirit will give a revelation to the church of how to respect, revere, honor, and love the man (or woman) of God in ministry. In turn, the servants of God in ministry will respect the spiritual sons and daughters whom God places in their life. Such an atmosphere of cordiality and respect will parallel Peter's reaction to the question Jesus posed in Matthew 16:15: "'Who do you say that I am?' Without hesitation, Peter answered, 'You are the Christ, the Son of the living God'" (KJV). Peter had a divine revelation of who Jesus was, just as the modern church needs a revelation of who Jesus is and whom He has sent to bless us.

Gift to the Body

A good question every church should ask is this: Who is the man (or woman) whom God has placed over our lives to lead, shepherd, and equip us? The Scriptures teach very precisely about this person's identity. According to Ephesians 4:11, this person is a gift to the body:

1) The pastor is a GIFT to the local church.

Generally, we give people gifts to show them we are grateful for them and value the role they play in our lives. God has given to each local church a gift because He loves us, appreciates us, and wants to show us how much He values us. In general, gifts are treasured. If a gift is of great value, it is often locked away in a safe place because it is special to the receiver. Spiritually, the pastor whom God has placed over our life to lead, shepherd, and equip us must be treasured and protected. God will reward His people for taking exceptionally good care of their pastor.

2) The pastor is the VISIONARY of the local church

In most cases, the visionary is the leader of the church, organization, or institution. It's the visionary who obtains God's vision for the local church. They delegate and drive the vision. In a church structure, the leader (i.e. the pastor) must see to it that the main reason of the church takes priority and overrides all other visions—for example, that of every other department. Every departmental vision must submit to the main vision of the church. If there is no submission, then the main vision will die or be fragmented. Leaders of various departments must understand their vision must submit to the main vision. The leadership of the church must know that they should not do anything in the body without first revealing it to the set man of the house. God always speaks to the set man of the house, and then He might confirm what He revealed to another in the house.

3) The pastor is the PROPHET for the local church

There is a misconception that a prophet is someone who foretells the future. This definition is too narrow. A prophet is better defined as "one who speaks for another." A true prophet, then, is a person who speaks for God, delivering a message God has ordained them to give. The person's essential role is to speak for God, regardless of whether it involves any predictions of the future. A prophet expresses the will of God in words and sometimes uses signs to back up those words and to demonstrate God's power behind them.

Scripture promises blessings to those who support prophets. "Believe in the Lord your God, and you shall be established; believe His prophets, and you shall prosper" (2 Chronicles 20:20, NKJV). Believing in God establishes you in your Christian faith, doctrines, and beliefs. Believing in God's prophet will cause you to prosper. God's prophet is the local pastor, the one who covers you. Among the many aspects of prospering are:

- Cause to blossom
- Cause to thrive
- To make progress
- To acquire wealth
- To achieve economic success
- To flourish
- To go ahead
- To succeed in an enterprise

To believe in the prophet means to believe in the person's God-given vision and dream, to believe in the word they preach and teach, and to believe that God called them. When you believe in the prophet of God (which is the man or woman of God), you will prosper.

Your Spiritual Father

Permit me to address specifically the men reading these words. Numerous young men and adult males in the house of God cannot understand why they are going through what they are going through, even after they make Jesus Christ their Lord. These men are coming into church with a generational curse over them—the curse of fatherlessness. They are overtaken by the spirit of rejection, anger, and frustration; many have no deep relationships with their spouse or children. The spirit of fatherlessness can be broken from the life of these fatherless children by coming under the covering of a spiritual father (the pastor). Timothy came under the covering of Paul, and Timothy became his spiritual son. Timothy's ministry flourished because of the covering over his life.

As a spiritual father, we do not replace natural fathers. A spiritual father can mentor, but a mentor cannot necessarily be a spiritual father. It is necessary for every born-again child of God to have spiritual parents. To understand spiritual truths and to get you to your spiritual destiny, you need spiritual parents in your life. The book of Matthew starts with the genealogy of Jesus Christ, meaning everybody needs to have a genealogy. Like we are birthed from the seed of a natural father, all of us are born again by the Word of God, but also through a man or woman of God.

Blessings of Love, Honor, and Respect

There are numerous examples in Scripture of the blessings that originate with showing love, honor, and respect for a spiritual father. In chapter 1, I recalled how Elisha received a double portion of Elijah's spirit, but I didn't mention Elisha served him for eight years before that took place. Joshua served Moses for more than 40 years and became his successor. Joshua received the anointing and grace from Moses to lead the children of Israel and take them across Jordan to the promised land.

A particularly moving story about the blessings from serving a prophet appears in 2 Kings 4:8-37, which talks about Elisha going to Shunem. A well-to-do woman lived there and urged him to stay for a meal. So whenever he came by, he stopped there to eat. This woman of God loved and feared Him, so whenever Elisha passed through Shunem, the woman would make bread for Elisha or bake him a cake. She would literally go looking for Elisha to see to it he was cared for and well fed.

One day she said to her husband, "I *perceive* that this is a holy man of God" (2 Kings 4:9, NASB, emphasis added). When she made this statement, she had already met Elisha and baked for him, but when she said, "I perceive," it signaled she had had a revelation of Elisha's identity. It is important to note her relationship with Elisha did not go the other way; she did not become familiar with him or dishonor or disrespect him. She even said to her husband, "Please, let us make a little walled upper chamber and let us set a bed for him there, and a table and a chair and a lampstand; and it shall be, when he comes to us, that he can turn in there" (2 Kings 4:10, NASB). So, they built and furnished the room, which became the breakthrough point of her miracles.

On one of Elisha's visits, he tells his servant, Gehazi, to call the Shunammite woman so he can ask her what he can do for her—such as speak to the king on her behalf, or maybe to the commander of the army. When she says she dwells among her own people, Elijah presses and asks what can be done for her. Gehazi tells him the woman has no son, and her husband is aged. So, Elisha prophesies that in a year she will give birth to a son, a claim so outrageous she said, "Man of God, do not lie to your maidservant!" (2 Kings 4:16, NASB). The result follows in verse 17: "But the woman conceived, and bore a son when the appointed time had come, of which Elisha had told her."

This was only the first miracle she experienced. After her son had grown, he fell sick one day and complained to his father about his head hurting. Tragically, he dies, but his mother went and laid him on Elisha's bed. After she goes to tell Elisha about it, he goes to his room, prays, and lays on the child—mouth to mouth, eyes to eyes, hands to hands—and the son's body becomes warm. But he's not quite alive, so Elisha walks back and forth in the house and again stretches out on him. The son sneezes seven times and opens his eyes. Elisha tells Gehazi to call the woman, and he presents her son to her. This is miracle number two.

But the story isn't over. In 2 Kings 8:1-6, Elisha tells the woman to return to the house of her birth because of the Lord calling for a famine on this land. This is the third miracle—the prophet gave her a forewarning about the coming famine that would last for seven years.

After it ends, the Shunammite woman left the land of the Philistines and came back home. The king was talking with Gehazi and asked the servant to tell him about the great things Elisha had done. As Gehazi was telling him about restoring the woman's son's life, she appeared and appealed to the king for her house and land. Gehazi verified her story. "So the king appointed a certain officer for her, saying, 'Restore all that was hers, and all the proceeds of the field from the day that she left the land until now'" (2 Kings 8:6, NASB).

This season of restoration was the fourth miracle she received. Initially, all this Shunammite woman did was bake bread for the man of God and see to it Elisha never went to bed hungry. After receiving the revelation that he was no ordinary man, she unlocked her miracles by serving him. Today we need to have a similar revelation; as we serve the man of God, we, too, will be able to unlock miracles. All that we need in life to be successful is in the spiritual womb of the man of God who gives a spiritual covering.

When Jesus sent out the 12 apostles, He told them, "He who receives you receives Me, and he who receives Me receives Him who sent Me. He who receives a prophet in the name of a prophet shall receive a prophet's reward. And he who receives a righteous man in the name of a righteous man shall receive a righteous man's reward. And whoever gives one of these little ones only a cup of cold water in the name of a disciple, assuredly, I say to you, he shall by no means lose his reward" (Matthew 10:40-42, NKJV). Such is the power of supporting God's servants!

Curse of Rebellion

When spiritual sons or daughters walk in rebellion, stubbornness, or disobedience toward their spiritual father or spiritual covering, they reap a curse. They are ignoring the clear instruction of the Word. Psalm 105:5 says, "Do not touch My anointed ones, and do My prophets no harm" (NKJV). Additionally, 1 Corinthians 16:22 adds, "If anyone does not love the Lord Jesus Christ, let him be accursed" (NKJV). Loving the Lord includes loving His pastors and prophets.

Now, every child of God is God's anointed, so we should not touch or hurt one another in thought, word, or deed. For the purpose of this teaching, I want to look at some verses from the perspective of the fivefold ministry, including ministerial leadership. Many preachers, teachers, and believers who walk and live in rebellion and stubbornness use these Scriptures to protect themselves from the partners or members whom they work with. However, Moses didn't write Genesis 4:8-16 to protect any pastor, teacher, or leader. It was purely written to explain the consequences that will occur when one oppresses, hurts, speaks evil of, or commits verbal or physical abuse to the servant of God—for example, a pastor, a teacher, or an apostle.

This passage talks about Cain killing Abel in a fit of jealousy after God didn't accept Cain's offering but did accept Abel's. After God tells Cain, "The voice of your brothers blood cries out to Me from the ground" (Genesis 4:10, NKJV), He tells Cain he is cursed from the earth, which has received Abel's blood. The lesson inherent in this passage is that Cain touched the anointed of God, and in response, the Lord cursed him and drove him out of the garden.

When you touch God's anointed, God curses you and drives you out of His presence.

This is also seen in Genesis 9:20-29, which relates the story of Noah after the great flood. He planted a vineyard, drank some of the wine produced from the grapes, and became drunk. After he passed out and laid uncovered inside his tent, his son, Ham, saw him naked and told his two brothers outside. The implication from Scripture here is that Ham was gossiping to his brothers about the incident and possibly lampooning his father because of his drunken stupor. But Shem and Japheth showed respect by taking a garment and laying it on their shoulders before walking in backward to cover Noah's body.

These actions carried serious consequences for Ham and great blessings for his brothers. "So Noah awoke from his wine, and knew what his younger son had done to him. Then he said 'Cursed be Canaan; a servant of servants he shall be to his brethren.' And he said 'Blessed be the Lord, the God of Shem, and may Canaan be his servant. May God enlarge Japheth, and may he dwell in the tents of Shem; and may Canaan be his servant'" (Genesis 9:24-27, NKJV).

In working relationships between spiritual fathers and sons or daughters, the children usually love, serve, and protect their spiritual fathers. In turn, the fathers mentor and give spiritual covering to their spiritual offspring. During this time of working together, each one can become familiar with the other, which can be very dangerous. When one becomes familiar with another, it is easy to lose respect for each other. Sometimes, submission to spiritual authority can become a challenge. The dangerous part of this close relationship is that the spiritual father and spiritual son or daughter get to know each other's strengths and weaknesses, and the dos and don'ts. When an issue or disagreement arises between the two parties, the challenge causes the spirit of familiarity to expose each other's weaknesses or to speak evil of one another.

Spiritual sons or daughters should never uncover the nakedness of their spiritual fathers (or parents) and never speak evil of them to anyone, whether amongst family members or friends. Uncovering their father's nakedness or speaking evil of him opens the door for the same kind of curse that rested on Ham to affect the child's life and family.

Choose the Blessing

Criticizing others, finding fault with their decisions, or making fun of them is such a common trait of our day and age that many don't see the seriousness of speaking against a spiritual father. Yet Scripture makes it clear we can receive blessings when we walk in obedience or curses if we walk in rebellion and stubbornness.

Here, a couple Old Testament examples are quite relevant. The first involves Miriam and Aaron, who spoke against Moses (see Numbers 12) because he had married a Cushite woman; the reference is often interpreted as someone from Ethiopia. When Miriam and Aaron did this, they broke their covenant with their brother Moses, committing two sins:

1) They spoke negatively about Moses's wife.

2) They spoke against his prophetic anointing and grace when they said, "Has the Lord indeed spoken only through Moses? Has He not spoken through us also?" (Number 12:2, NKJV). Not only did this arouse the Lord's anger, but He then struck Miriam with leprosy. The reason is because Moses was God's voice and chosen leader of the children of Israel.

It is important to know no matter who we are, we cannot rise up against God's appointed man (or woman) whom God has chosen to lead His people. When God chooses a man, God gives him the vision, leadership, grace, and anointing to lead His people. God will not speak to any others in the group of leaders. Aaron and Miriam wanted the congregation to know that God spoke through them and that God called all three of them (Moses, Aaron, and Miriam). To correct the matter, God said, in effect, "If there was another prophet beside Moses, I would have let you know."

Verse 15 describes Miriam being shut out of the camp for seven days while the children of Israel did not move. When spiritual sons and daughters or other leaders stand up against their spiritual father or another leader in rebellion, it angers God. He releases a curse and stops the flow of His anointing so there is no movement. The lesson of Numbers 12 is that spiritual sons and daughters should not stand up against their spiritual fathers. If they do, they open the door for a curse (i.e. leprosy or other sickness) to come on their life. Rebellion against the spiritual father or the set person of God can also stop the flow of the supernatural or the church from moving to the next level.

Then, in Numbers 16, Korah, Dathan, and Abiram—the latter two long-time opponents of Moses who tried to persuade the Israelites to return to Egypt—joined 250 leaders of the congregation in opposition to Moses and Aaron. "You take too much upon yourselves, for all the congregation is holy, every one of them, and the Lord is among them. Why then do you exalt yourselves above the assembly of the Lord?" (Number 16:3, NKJV). In other words, Korah and his team were challenging the leadership anointing and grace on the lives of Moses and Aaron.

While they knew the Lord had appointed Moses, the spirits of envy and rebellion made them behave that way. We cannot fight God's plan or God's will whenever He appoints leaders over our lives. The sin that Korah and the others committed was wanting to function in the priesthood. It is reminiscent of the story of King Saul. When Samuel delayed coming, Saul took the place of a high priest and offered the sacrifice. But Samuel told him, "You have done foolishly. You have not kept the commandment of the Lord your God, which He commanded you. For now the Lord would have established your kingdom over Israel forever. But now your kingdom shall not continue" (1 Samuel 13:13-14, NKJV).

For Korah and the other 250 men who rebelled against Moses, the Bible says the earth beneath them opened up and swallowed Korah, his family, and the other men and their families. That's some serious punishment! We should learn from this story to not be in rebellion against the spiritual father or other leader God places over you. In addition, recognize your rebellion won't affect only yourself. The entire family suffers and goes through pain, hardship, and death because of such foolishness.

A Word for Fathers

Fatherhood is affirmed as a state of having one or more children. Fathers play a pivotal role in their family; often the success of the father determines the success of the entire family. If the family is going through struggles and poverty, it can well be because of the father. As earthly fathers, it's important to check our foundation. The foundation upon which we build determines our future. As Psalm 11:3 asks, "If the foundations are destroyed, what can the righteous do?" (NKJV).

Where we are today is because of our foundation, just as where our children will be one day will be because of the foundation we lay for them. As fathers, many of us are who we are because of the foundation our grandparents have laid. If you are not happy with your present state, then deal with the foundation. If we don't deal with ourselves, we are going to produce bad fruit.

Our responsibilities as fathers are to provide, protect, discipline, mentor, and teach. The roles we play are father, leader, prophet, priest, and king. If we can demonstrate this right, then our next generation will be blessed. Anyone can make a child, but it takes a real man to be a father and a dad. A good father makes all the difference in a child's life. He is a pillar of strength, support, and discipline. His work is endless and often thankless. But in the end, it shows in the sound and well-adjusted children he (and his wife) raise.

CHAPTER FIVE

Spiritual Fathering

We live in a fatherless generation. This reality is reflected by looking at the homes in our communities and the children who are part of our ministry. A number of children in our churches are being brought up by single mothers, grandparents, aunts and uncles, or orphanages and other institutions. Too often, biological fathers are absent from our homes. Statistics for South Africa reveal:

- As of 2017, there were 2.8 million orphans in the nation. That includes children without a biological mother, father, or both parents and is equivalent to 14 percent of all children in the country.[1]
- Three thousand children are abandoned each year.[2]
- Nearly 62 percent of children under the age of 18 live without their father, giving us one of the highest rates of fatherlessness in the world. Not surprisingly, of the 2.1 million crimes committed in 2016, males ages 15-34 were the most likely group to commit crimes.[3]

This crisis is not restricted to Third World countries. In mid-2020 in the affluent United States, the National Fatherhood Initiative said more than one-in-four children, or 19.7 million, were living without a father in the home.[4] The consequences can be seen in the statistics compiled in one recent study of America:

- 63 percent of youth suicides come from fatherless homes.
- 70 percent of juveniles come from fatherless homes.

- 80 percent of rapists motivated by displaced anger come from fatherless homes.
- 85 percent of children with behavioral problems come from fatherless homes.
- 90 percent of homeless children come from fatherless homes.[5]

Poverty, poor education, antisocial behavior, and disrupted employment in life are all the result of fathers being absent from the home. Broken people breed broken families, broken families breed broken communities, and broken communities breed a broken nation. Broken families also breed a broken church.

The spirit of fatherlessness is prevailing forcefully in South Africa and other nations of the world. This is why Malachi 4:6—which I quoted early in this book—is such a powerful verse in Scripture. One of the spirits the prophet Elijah functioned in was the spirit of fatherhood. He foretold of how, before the coming of our Lord Jesus Christ a second time, God is going to release the spirit of fatherhood upon the earth, restoring the hearts of the fathers to their sons, and sons (and daughters) to their fathers. The verse concludes: "Lest I come and strike the earth with a curse" (NKJV).

The Curse

There are a number of curses on the earth in the 21st century, but one of the greatest curses is the orphan spirit, which I mentioned in chapter 3. Millions of men, women, and children are enslaved by this spirit because they were not raised by a father or because they do not have a fatherly covering. Many men, women, and children in church, even when they are born again and love Jesus, are enslaved by this spirit. Even though they are part of a congregation and profess to worship God, they have not recognized the father in the house or come under the fatherly covering of the man of God.

To amplify what I said earlier about this spirit, some traits of those who either carry it or are enslaved by it display these traits:

1) They suffer with feelings of abandonment, rejection, and disappointment and experience depression, discouragement, and feelings of hopelessness. Because of abandonment, they want to be left alone, like being lonely, withdraw when in a crowd, and feel forsaken—that nobody loves them or notices them. They give up easily, don't put up a fight, and often start something but give up and do not continue to the end.

2) Because of abandonment and rejection, they are driven by the search for significance. Because they have never been affirmed by a father while growing up, they constantly strive to succeed. They have a quest to elevate themselves among others so that they can feel good about themselves. Those who are driven by the spirit of the orphan most times are driven by personal ambition rather than the Holy Spirit. Such ambition can be very self-destructive.

3) They are always in competition with others. Because they have not been affirmed by a father, they work hard to prove themselves to others. But in trying to prove themselves, they find themselves competing with others. This is neither healthy for the individual nor for their interpersonal relationships. Few people want to be friends with someone who is always competing with them.

4) They are always looking for approval and recognition. Those who carry the orphan spirit have a huge void in their hearts, which only God can heal. Their pain is so deep that they always look for temporal

relief by getting people to notice them in order to receive accolades. As long as they don't allow God to heal their woundedness, they will always be seeking the approval of men and women.

5) They don't know how to emotionally connect with others. While they may know how to dispense a task, they don't know how to emotionally connect with those around them. Those who carry this spirit don't know how to connect with their wives, and because they have not been fathered, they don't know how to connect with their sons or daughters. This is an incredibly sad and lonely place to be as a parent, particularly considering the fact the orphan spirit will likely reproduce itself in the children.

6) They don't feel good about themselves. Even though they might have high accomplishments, they suffer from low self-esteem. They try to desperately compensate for this self-disdain through their achievements. Even though they might look good and have a great public personality, they hate themselves and often engage in self-condemnation.

Rejecting Authority

Those who carry the spirit of the orphan also don't know how to submit to authority. Most believers know how to honor, love, and respect God, but they do not know how to honor, love, and respect the man of God. Boys who have been raised without a father often grow up demonstrating a "macho" nature to compensate for their insecurity, stemming from the lack of a male image at home. When they come into the kingdom of God, many come in with a macho spirit. As a result, it becomes hard for them to submit to or accept correction or discipline. They often become aggressive and angry.

To anyone who struggles with this hindrance, I proclaim: You do not have to live with the orphan spirit any longer! You can break the rule of the spirit over your life by making God the Father over your life and by coming under the covering of spiritual parents. As Jesus told the apostles when He sent them out to minister, "He who receives you receives Me, and he who receives Me receives Him who sent Me. He who receives a prophet in the name of a prophet shall receive a prophet's reward. And he who receives a righteous man in the name of a righteous man shall receive a righteous man's reward" (Matthew 10:40-41, NKJV).

Respect for those God sends to His body is a serious issue. The reason men and women of God are not honored, revered, loved, and respected is the spirit of familiarity. Familiarity means to know someone very well and in such a way as to cause you to lose your admiration, respect, and sense of awe for that person. Yet familiarity is the greatest block to the anointing and the greatest block to receiving God's power from God's man (or woman). No matter how great and big the gift of God is, it is neutralized by the spirit of familiarity. As I mentioned earlier, Jesus was the greatest healer, teacher, and evangelist of all time, but in His hometown, He could not do any mighty miracles because of the spirit of familiarity.

This habit runs directly counter to the instruction of Scripture. Paul advised the church at Corinth, "Therefore, from now on, we regard no one according to the flesh. Even though we have known Christ according to the flesh, yet now we know Him thus no longer" (2 Corinthians 5:16, NKJV). Paul also wrote to the church at Ephesus, "But to each one of us grace was given according to the measure of Christ's gift. Therefore He says: 'When He ascended on high, He led captivity captive, and gave gifts to men'" (Ephesians 4:7-8, NKJV).

Don't miss the significance of that last phrase: *The Almighty gave gifts to human beings.*

God gave the body of Christ gifts to teach, train, mentor, and equip them for the work of ministry and to bring this body into a place of maturity in Jesus Christ and the full knowledge of His Son. The challenge we face in modern times is that the body of Christ lacks the revelation of the enormous value of the treasure God has given His people.

In the previous chapter, I mentioned Matthew 16:15 and Peter's response to Jesus's question: "Who do you say that I am?"—that He was indeed the Son of God. But what I didn't include was how Jesus answered Peter: "Blessed are you, Simon Bar-Jonah, for flesh and blood has not revealed this to you, but My Father who is in heaven" (Matthew 16:17, NKJV).

In these verses, we learn about the power of perception. Perception is to know, identify, become aware of, recognize, and discern by the means of your senses, to perceive by observation. Jesus was telling Peter human insight did not reveal this truth; His Father gave him the ability to see more than what Peter's eyes could see. This was a divine revelation. Revelation means the act of revealing something not realized before. Something that was once sealed or closed is now disclosed.

Peter had a revelation of the full identity of Jesus. Sure, in human terms, He was the son of Joseph and Mary, but He was also the Son of the living God. Although born in a manger in the humblest of circumstances in Bethlehem, he existed before the foundations of the world were framed. This is the same kind of revelation the Shunammite woman had in 2 Kings 4:8-9, which I mentioned in the last chapter. She was saying, in effect, "I have had a revelation: this is not just any man—He is a holy man of God. He is not just an ordinary man; he is my holy man. He is not just a prophet; I realize he carries my destiny. He is not just an ordinary man of God; he carries in his womb my promise and my future."

This woman came to the full understanding that when she came under Elisha's covering, she came under God's grace. When she connected to him, the supernatural anointing on his life would overflow onto her. What revelation do you have about your man of God? Your revelation will predicate your destiny. Remember:

1) He is your GIFT
2) He is your FATHER
3) He is your PROPHET
4) He is your VISIONARY

Becoming Children

Both my wife and I have spent nearly four decades in ministry. We have been through good times and bad. We have been through hardship and struggles. There were great and exciting moments. The greatest lesson I have learned is that you cannot build God's kingdom on elders, leaders, and workers; you need to build the kingdom on sons and daughters. How did I learn these lessons? Through church splits. When I was going through one struggle, I heard the Holy Spirit distinctly say: "If you do not raise sons and build on sons, then everything you build will crumble." So, I researched and found that the biblical pattern of God was Father and Son. When God created the universe, he created with Father and Son (and Holy Spirit).

Even though I have quoted some of the following passages before, they merit repeating here because of their application to the principle of fathers and sons, all from the NKJV translation.

- Genesis 1:26: "Let Us make man in Our image."
- John 1:1-3: "In the beginning was the Word and the Word was with God and the Word was God. He was

in the beginning with God. All things were made through Him, and without Him nothing was made that was made."

- Genesis 49:1: "And Jacob called his sons and said, 'Gather together, that I may tell you what shall befall you in the last days.'"
- Matthew 10:1: "And when He had called His twelve disciples to Him, He gave them power over unclean spirits, to cast them out, and to heal all kinds of sickness and all kinds of disease." When Jesus birthed His ministry, He called to himself 12 sons. When Paul wanted to establish his ministry, he called Timothy (2 Timothy 1:2) and Titus (Titus 1:4) as sons.
- Malachi 4:6: "And he will turn the hearts of the fathers to the children, and the hearts of the children to their fathers, lest I come and strike the earth with a curse." In the end times, it is God's desire to establish His kingdom on earth through fathers and sons (and daughters).
- 1 Corinthians 4:15: For though you might have ten thousand instructors in Christ, yet you do not have many fathers; for in Christ Jesus I have begotten you through the gospel."
- Romans 8:15-16: "For you did not receive the spirit of bondage again to fear, but you received the Spirit of adoption by whom we cry out, 'Abba, Father.' The Spirit Himself bears witness with our spirit that we are children of God."

Functions of a Spiritual Father

The roles of a spiritual father are to raise up sons and daughters spiritually while nurturing and protecting them. The spiritual parent will pour out knowledge, wisdom, counsel, and blessing to his children. The spiritual father's primary goal is to make the son or daughter successful in knowing the Lord and fulfilling the call of God on their life. It is important for a father to spend time with his children and enjoy precious moments together—not out of obligation, but because they are family.

To become a spiritual son or daughter, these children must be willing to birth into their spirit the father's DNA. In chapter 1, I mentioned two leading traits of spiritual sons and daughters: their spiritual pursuits and them possessing the father's DNA. Here are several more:

Sign 1: You will know them by their passion

True sons and daughters will have a hunger and a passion that they act on. Since they pursue growth, learning, and development, they position themselves to learn and grow in everything they do. One thing I have learned through years in ministry is that you cannot teach passion; this quality must be stirred up from within. I can read the Word, fast, and pray. I can motivate you and inspire you. But I cannot give you passion. Sons and daughters reveal themselves because they seek out fathers to learn from, and they are willing to do whatever it takes them to get there. Pursuit tells you who someone really is.

Sign 2: You will know them by their heart to serve

Sons and daughters have no agenda except to add value to the father's ministry. They don't push their own resume, and they don't chase titles. They don't compete with the father or other children; they just want to see others succeed. They have no agenda but to bless others.

Sign 3: You will know them by how they handle authority

How a person responds to authority is one of the greatest marks of how they will go through life. Authority is God's environment to break rebellion, pride, and stubbornness out of our lives. When we respond correctly to authority, we give greater room for promotion, blessing, and overall growth. There are talented and qualified people in ministry, but while leading, can they also submit to authority? Too many who pursue a career in ministry are consumed with their own dreams and missions. They want to lead but have no desire to submit to a spiritual father (or mother) or come under any kind of authority. Every son or daughter has their own dream, and as they serve, God will help their dream to come to pass.

Sign 4: You will know them by how they handle correction

One of God's greatest tests for a true son or daughter is how they handle correction (Hebrews 12:6). Correction is usually the biggest and final test in the processing of a child's heart. Correction is uncomfortable. It reveals a son or daughter's heart and attitude. Fathers don't correct children to put them to shame or bring humiliation to them, but to better their character. Correction helps children to work on the blind spots in their lives. If a son or daughter cannot take correction, then they are not a true son or daughter and will never be able to serve because humility is not part of their character.

Sign 5: You will know them over the test of time

Relationship, trust and credibility are built gradually. Seasoned time will tell if a person is serious about walking as a true son or daughter of the kingdom. In time, you are likely to find that many sons and daughters with great potential fade away because they cannot stand the test of time. This is all part of the journey.

CHAPTER SIX

Honoring Fatherhood

Though Jesus spoke the following words nearly 2,000 years ago, they are still the subject of controversy and disagreements in the church, regardless of denominational affiliation or background. Like all His words, the Matthew 23:8-11 passage causes us to stop and catch our breath. These words have raised great concern for many, as they should for all of us. We must take seriously the words and teachings of our Lord. And these words seem to support all who do not believe the teachings about spiritual fathers and sons and daughters in the church:

> **Matthew 23:8-11**: *"But you, do not be called 'Rabbi'; for One is your Teacher, the Christ, and you are all brethren. Do not call anyone on earth your father; for One is your Father, He who is in heaven. And do not be called teachers; for One is your Teacher, the Christ. But he who is greatest among you shall be your servant" (NKJV).*

Many have asked me what I have to say about Jesus's direct command in these verses. When we look at these verses solely and without the benefit of any further study, it would appear on the surface the teaching of spiritual fathers and sons and daughters is not biblical—that Jesus forbids us to call anyone on earth "Father." But I encourage you to consider the following with me as we delve further into the Scriptures.

The God-Given Gift of Fatherhood

Fatherhood belongs to God. He is our heavenly Father and is to be known and adored as Father. From Him all creation emanates; from Him all things came into being. Numerous Scriptures speak of Him as a Father or offering a father's guidance. A few examples:

- Psalm 103:13: "The Lord is like a father to his children, tender and compassionate to those who fear him" (NLT).
- Deuteronomy 1:30-31: "The Lord your God, who goes before you, He will fight for you, according to all He did for you in Egypt before your eyes, and in the wilderness where you saw how the Lord your God carried you, as a man carries his son, in all the way that you went until you came to this place" (NKJV).
- Proverbs 3:11-12: "My son, do not despise the chastening of the Lord, nor detest His correction; for whom the Lord loves He corrects, just as a father the son in whom he delights" (NKJV).
- 2 Corinthians 6:18: "I will be a Father to you, and you shall be My sons and daughters, says the Lord Almighty" (NKJV).
- Hebrews 12:7: "Endure hardship as discipline; God is treating you as his children. For what children are not disciplined by their father?" (NIV).

Fatherhood is an honor that belongs first and foremost to God. Therefore, fatherhood is a gift—and a responsibility—from God. He gave it to us for specific purposes and reasons. Fatherhood is the ability to reproduce, provide for, protect, and raise. Each one of us came into this world through a biological father. Furthermore, others have had the privilege of raising children who are not their biological children and fulfilling the role and responsibilities of being a stepfather.

A Closer Look

Taking the words of Jesus in Matthew 28:8-11 without consideration or context can pose several challenges. Here are three to consider:

1) Is Christ forbidding us to call our biological father or stepfather "father?"
2) Is Christ forbidding the practice of calling someone father, including Father Abraham?
3) Is Christ forbidding us to call anyone father, even a spiritual father?

To examine these questions individually, let's look first at whether Christ is forbidding us from calling our biological father or stepfather "father." If this is true, then we all have sinned since childhood in this regard. Furthermore, how do we reconcile the Scriptures that admonish us regarding biological parents and the need to show them honor?

Here, Ephesians 6:1-4 offers relevant advice: "Children, obey your parents in the Lord, for this is right. 'Honor your father and mother,' which is the first commandment with promise: 'that it may be well with you and you may live long on the earth.' And you, fathers, do not provoke your children to wrath, but bring them up in the training and admonition of the Lord" (NKJV).

The apostle Paul admonishes the Ephesians and all believers concerning the relationship of honor between children and their parents. He teaches that by the Spirit of God, children should obey and honor their parents. The Word of God does not contradict itself. The role and responsibility of father and mother is designated. By the command of God, children are to honor their fathers and mothers. In verse 4, Paul highlights the responsibility of fathers: to raise their children in the right way and attitude. Herein is the role and responsibility of a father, as well as the obedience and honor to a father (and mother) God expects. This is a quality rooted in a heart of genuine honor and obedience, including how children should address their parents.

As a side note, remember the Bible declares that all Scripture is inspired by God and cannot be broken. As 2 Timothy 3:16-17 says, "All Scripture is given by inspiration of God, and is profitable for doctrine, for reproof, for correction, for instruction in righteousness, that the man of God may be complete, thoroughly equipped for every good work" (NKJV).

The apostle Peter affirms this view in 2 Peter 1:20-21: "Knowing this first, that no prophecy of Scripture is of any private interpretation, for prophecy never came by the will of man, but holy men of God spoke as they were moved by the Holy Spirit" (NKJV).

Therefore, if it is wrong to call anyone "father," then the apostle Paul has incorrectly admonished us to honor our father and mother. Notice how Paul writes to the Ephesians under the inspiration of the Holy Spirit and speaks to children to obey their parents because it is right; we are to honor our parents because it is a command of God. Notice how both parents are mentioned—fatherhood and motherhood. God commands honor to these roles and to the persons carrying these responsibilities.

Paul elaborates on how honoring your father and mother is the first commandment with a promise, one that comes with a great reward: that it will go well with you and that you may live long on the earth. This speaks of the quality of your life. So, when we honor our parents, there is the promise of blessing. Obeying God's commandments brings blessings. When we honor fatherhood and motherhood, I believe we tap into God's promised and commanded blessing.

As part of his instruction, Paul also admonishes fathers not to provoke their children to wrath. You have likely seen this in action—a father who constantly criticizes, nit-picks, and belittles a child until the frustrated youngster shuts down and becomes withdrawn, only to flower into full-fledged rebellion as a teenager. Instead, Paul says fathers are to bring up their children in the training and admonition of the Lord. Fathers have an honor and responsibility as well in God's sight.

We can see from the Scripture it is not wrong to refer to someone as "father." Indeed, Scripture commands us to honor our biological father and mother in this way. We are to bring honor to them, not dishonor. Addressing your biological parents as "father" and "mother" and praising them to others whilst you obey them is an honorable thing.

The Honor of a Father

According to the book of Malachi, the role of a father carries great honor. Look at the first chapter: "A son honors his father, and a servant his master. If then I am the Father, where is My honor? And if I am a Master, where is My reverence? says the Lord of hosts to you priests who despise My name. Yet you say, 'In what way have we despised Your name?'" (Malachi 1:6, NKJV).

In this verse, we read of God asking the priest concerning His honor as Father. Notice the Lord says, "A son honors his Father." The Lord then asks, in effect, "If I am the Father, where is My honor?" We can understand from this statement it is biblically fitting to honor a father. A son is to honor his father, just as a servant reverences his master. God teaches us to honor our father and to show reverence for those who are in positions over us. This is a key value of the kingdom of God, where we are to display honor and reverence towards a person's role and responsibility. We cannot claim to honor the heavenly Father and dishonor our earthly fathers.

This brings us to the second question: Is Christ forbidding the practice of calling someone father, including Father Abraham? This is a key question, considering the Scripture calls Abraham by the following honorable titles:

- Father of many nations
- Father of faith
- Father of us all

The first title appears in Genesis 17:4-5: "As for Me, behold, My covenant is with you, and you shall be a father of many nations. No longer shall your name be called Abram, but your name shall be Abraham; for I have made you a father of many nations" (NKJV).

This is where God changed Abram's name—which meant "exalted father"—to Abraham, meaning "father of many nations." God gave Abraham a blessing and responsibility before his wife had borne him any children. God called a man who was not yet a father "a father of many nations." We know this covenant included biological and spiritual fatherhood. We see in the New Testament how Abraham's spiritual fatherhood extends to all who believe in Christ: "And if you are Christ's, then you are Abraham's seed, and heirs according to the promise" (Galatians 3:29, NKJV).

We know we are not Abraham's biological offspring. However, by God's covenant calling, all who believe in Jesus Christ are Abraham's spiritual children. Therefore, Abraham is our father in faith. You and I cannot even say the name "Abraham" without calling him "father of many nations," for that is what his name means. If Christ is forbidding us to call anyone "father," then it would be wrong to call Abram by his covenant name, Abraham.

Furthermore, the Scripture distinctly declares Abraham's fatherhood over all believers: "Therefore it is of faith that it might be according to grace, so that the promise might be sure to all the seed, not only to those who are of the law, but also to those who are of the faith of Abraham, who is the father of us all (as it is written, 'I have made you a father of many nations') in the presence of Him whom he believed—God, who gives life to the dead and calls those things which do not exist as though they did" (Romans 4:16-17, NKJV).

We see by the authority of Scripture that Abraham is the father of all who have faith in God through Christ Jesus. The Scriptures are not in contradiction to Jesus, and Jesus is not in contradiction to the Scriptures.

Abraham is also called the father of circumcision. He received circumcision as the sign of his covenant with God. However, he was declared righteous before he was circumcised. This made him father of the circumcised and uncircumcised. As Romans 4:10-12 says:

"How then was it accounted? While he was circumcised, or uncircumcised? Not while circumcised, but while uncircumcised. And he received the sign of circumcision, a seal of the righteousness of the faith which he had while still uncircumcised, that he might be the father of all those who believe, though they are uncircumcised, that righteousness might be imputed to them also, and the father of circumcision to those who not only are of the circumcision, but who also walk in the steps of the faith which our father Abraham had while still uncircumcised" (NKJV).

The honor of fatherhood is great. Since God bestowed it on Abraham, we are to call and honor him as God designated. Thus, it cannot be forbidden to address him as "father." The Scripture admonishes us to show this honor and affection to our biological father and here to our spiritual father, Abraham.

So, what is Christ really dealing with when he said this? I believe He was warning us of something deeper—something more dangerous than merely calling someone father. He is warning us against satanic fatherhood. This is what we read in John 8, where Jesus dealt with the Pharisees and warned that they were not of God. Abraham's true fatherhood is from God and magnifies God's fatherhood, whilst there is a fatherhood that is satanic and ungodly.

Abraham's Seed and Satan's

John 8:37-44: "'I know that you are Abraham's descendants, but you seek to kill Me, because My word has no place in you. I speak what I have seen with My Father, and you do what you have seen with your father.' They answered and said to Him, 'Abraham is our father Jesus said to them, 'If you were Abraham's children, you would do the works of Abraham. But now you seek to kill Me, a Man who has told you the truth which I heard from God. Abraham did not do this. You do the deeds of your father.' Then they said to Him, 'We were not born of fornication; we have one Father—God.' Jesus said to them, 'If God were your Father, you would love Me, for I proceeded forth and came from God; nor have I come of Myself, but He sent Me. Why do you not understand My speech? Because you are not able to listen to My word. You are of [your] father the devil, and the desires of your father you want to do. He was a murderer from the beginning, and does not stand in the truth, because there is no truth in him. When he speaks a lie, he speaks from his own resources, for he is a liar and the father of it.'" (NKJV).

Here is the challenge of fatherhood: Jesus is the Son of God—the heavenly Father. Jesus confronts the descendants of Abraham, who is the father of faith, father of circumcision, and father of those of faith in Christ. What Jesus says challenges the Jews who are listening to Him. If they were Abraham's descendants, and Abraham was truly their father, they would not do the things they are doing. Here we see that true, comprehensive fatherhood is more than just biological; it contains a spiritual dimension.

Jesus further challenged them, pointing out that even though they were Abraham's seed, their hearts and their submission was to another. By identifying their other father, He exposed them. He was not only speaking about their natural biological father but their spiritual father.

By standing in direct contrast to the Son of God and the heavenly Father, Jesus was declaring they were of their father, the devil. Did you know Satan has fatherhood over people? He influences them, covers them, and persuades them to do his will. Imagine that they were not under the Abrahamic fatherhood, which comes from God. Even though they were Abraham's biological seed, they had moved away spiritually and come under a different spiritual father. They were now following Satan's desires and were under the devil's fatherhood and influence. Many do not recognize there is a spiritual battle for fatherhood. Fatherhood is under attack on every level—biological, adoptive, and spiritual, by a fatherhood that is ungodly, unholy, and satanic. Beware of this danger!

God has given us biological, adoptive, and spiritual fatherhood so we can be fruitful, multiply, replenish the earth, have dominion over it, and subdue it. Godly parents raise godly children. Step- or foster parents care and love children through a spirit of adoption to bring covering and blessing to the orphan. Spiritual fatherhood brings blessings of faith, promise, and discipline in righteousness.

Unfortunately, the men Jesus was speaking to were men under the spirit and fatherhood of Satan. When you understand this revelation, you will understand Jesus's words in Matthew 23, because the scribes and Pharisees were not under the fatherhood of God that had come through the fatherhood of Abraham, but they were under the fatherhood of Satan. They rebelled against God, so Jesus gives a command not to call anyone on earth father who is in rebellion to God.

Finally, we have the question: Is Jesus forbidding us from calling anyone father, even a spiritual father? Perhaps we can ask another question: Is there such a role as a spiritual father? To answer that, let's consider Paul's writings to the Corinthians.

Paul's Paternal Care

I start with 1 Corinthians 4:14-17, which contains the verse I have quoted previously about not having many fathers in Christ:

"I do not write these things to shame you, but as my beloved children I warn you. For though you might have ten thousand instructors in Christ, yet you do not have many fathers; for in Christ Jesus I have begotten you through the gospel. Therefore I urge you, imitate me. For this reason I have sent Timothy to you, who is my beloved and faithful son in the Lord, who will remind you of my ways in Christ, as I teach everywhere in every church" (NKJV).

In all his writings, Paul writes with love from his heart. He often cared for the churches as a pastor and an apostle, but most importantly as a father. He saw himself in this latter role with a seriousness and responsibility. Here we see how he clearly declares the Corinthians his beloved children. He affirms that though they may have many instructors and preachers teaching them the Word of God, they didn't have spiritual fathers. Paul fulfilled that key role, having begotten them in the Lord. Paul founded the church in Corinth and was responsible for it. They all were directly or indirectly saved through the gospel under Paul's ministry through his prayers. As their spiritual father, he urged them to imitate him.

Was Paul wrong to see himself this way? Was he sinning by referring to himself this way? I don't think so. Paul further continues with this revelation of fathers and sons by promising to send Timothy, "who is my beloved and faithful son in the Lord." These words leave no doubt of the reality of father and son in the Lord. Remember Paul taught we should obey our parents in the Lord. I believe he included spiritual parenting in this category. While Timothy was not Paul's biological son, he was his spiritual son. If Paul can call Timothy his "son," would it be wrong for Timothy to refer to Paul as "father?"

Paul raised Timothy spiritually, writing him two letters in which Paul honored Timothy. Paul opens his first letter (1 Timothy 2): "To Timothy, a true son in the faith: Grace, mercy, and peace from God our Father and Jesus Christ our Lord." These words are nearly identical to the greeting in 2 Timothy 1:2, except in the second he calls Timothy a "beloved" son. In 1 Timothy 1:18, Paul starts the conclusion to the chapter with: "This charge I commit to you, son Timothy, according to the prophecies previously made concerning you, that by them you may wage the good warfare." All these exchanges are evidence of the love, care, tenderness, and affirmation that flow between father and son, a direct parallel to the Father and Son of creation.

Conclusion

I really believe the honor and respect in a family should be in the church as well because it exemplifies the DNA of our God. We are to honor fatherhood, motherhood, brotherhood, and sisterhood in the church and in God's kingdom. This is illustrated in the fifth chapter of Paul's first letter to Timothy: "Do not rebuke an older man, but exhort him as a father, younger men as brothers, older women as mothers, younger women as sisters, with all purity. Honor widows who are really widows. But if any widow has children or grandchildren, let them first learn to show piety at home and to repay their parents; for this is good and acceptable before God" (1 Timothy 5:1-4, NKJV).

The church is a family and is to be cared for, nourished, led, and governed as such. There is a godly spiritual fatherhood; we are to be beneficiaries of this care and love that is on earth, expressing the fatherhood of our heavenly Father. So, Christ is not forbidding the core value of the kingdom of God that is testified throughout Scripture, from the Old Testament to the New Testament. He is warning against and forbidding satanic fatherhood. May we understand these truths as we live under the fatherhood blessing given by our heavenly Father.

CHAPTER SEVEN

The Blessing

The Jewish people have excelled throughout history in the fields of medicine, literature, science, the arts, and much more. There is no rational explanation for this, other than that this success is a direct result of the supernatural power of the prophetic blessing that appears in Genesis 12:1-3: "Now the Lord had said to Abram: 'Get out of your country, from your family and from your father's house, to a land that I will show you. I will make you a great nation; I will bless you and make your name great; and you shall be a blessing. I will bless those who bless you, and I will curse him who curses you; and in you all the families of the earth shall be blessed'" (NKJV).

Let's look at a few numbers. As of 2020, there were an estimated 16.6 million Jewish people worldwide within a population of 7.8 billion, or 0.002 percent of all people. Yet since 1947, in that minuscule proportion of the world's inhabitants, the Jewish people have been awarded the largest percentage (27 percent) of Nobel prizes—even after the Holocaust destroyed one-third of their numbers. The logical answer for this historical accomplishment is the power of prophetic blessing that the fathers and mothers have spoken over their beloved children every Sabbath throughout the generations.

The Jewish people have not only released the blessing, but they have also received the blessing and carried it into their lives. In accomplishing every word spoken over them, they are a shining example of the power in a father's blessing. Isaac blessed Jacob and Esau, and both blessings came true exactly as Isaac spoke them. Because of Abraham's obedience to the call of God on his life, God pronounces a blessing over Abraham and his future, promising that He will bless him. God will make Abraham the father of a nation from which salvation of the world will come—a promise that God fulfilled.

The Three Sons

We see the promise to Abraham start to play out in the life of Abraham's son, Isaac, and his sons, Esau and Jacob. Genesis 27 begins: "Now it came to pass, when Isaac was old and his eyes were so dim that he could not see, that he called Esau his older son and said to him, 'My son.' And he answered him, 'Here I am.' Then he said, 'Behold now, I am old. I do not know the day of my death. Now therefore, please take your weapons, your quiver and your bow, and go out to the field and hunt game for me. And make me savory food, such as I love, and bring it to me that I may eat, that my soul may *bless you* before I die'" (Genesis 27:1-4, NKJV, emphasis added).

Anyone who is familiar with Scripture knows what happens next: Jacob's mother, Rebekah, who favors her younger son, plots with Jacob to fool Isaac in order to obtain his father's spoken blessing because she appreciates the power inherent in a father's blessing. So she prepares the kind of meal Isaac likes and helps Jacob disguise himself before he takes it to his father.

Once Jacob has tricked his father into believing he is Esau, the elderly man says: "'Surely, the smell of my son is like the smell of a field which the Lord has blessed. Therefore may God give you of the dew of heaven, of the fatness of the earth, and plenty of grain and wine. Let peoples serve you, and nations bow down to you. Be master over your brethren, and let your mother's sons bow down to you. Cursed be everyone who curses you, and *blessed be those who bless you!*" (Genesis 27:27-29, NKJV, emphasis added).

As with all subterfuge, Jacob's deceit surfaces when Esau comes in with a plate of savory food and asks for his father's blessing: "Then Isaac trembled exceedingly, and said, 'Who? Where is the one who hunted game and brought it to me? I ate all of it before you came, and I have blessed him—and *indeed he shall be blessed*.' When Esau heard the words of his father, he cried with an exceedingly great and bitter cry, and said to his father, 'Bless me—me also, O my father!' But he said, 'Your brother came with deceit and has taken away your blessing'" (Genesis 27:32-35, NKJV, emphasis added).

Esau knew the power of a blessing, so he begged his father for one as well, but the blessing did not come. The spoken blessing could not be revoked, transferred, or surpassed. No power on earth—no king, no president, and no prime minister—can ever change the power of the prophetic blessing.

Jacob's Sons

Years later, Jacob calls his 12 sons together so he "may tell you what shall befall you in the last days" (Genesis 49:1, NKJV). Jacob knows he is in the final stages of life, so he summons his sons to his bedside to impart a prophetic blessing over each of them. Genesis 49 paints a stunning, prophetic masterpiece of the future of Israel, her people, and of Christ's redemption and His return.

Hebrews 11:21 captures the scene: "By faith Jacob, when he was dying, blessed each of the sons of Joseph, and worshiped, leaning on the top of his staff" (NKJV). Jacob is sitting at the edge of the bed; his 12 sons are with him in the room. The sons know their father, a spiritual giant and part of the nation's three-fold patriarchal cord, and he speaks forth their future as the 12 torches of Israel. He begins with the eldest son: "'Reuben, you are my firstborn, my might and the beginning of my strength, the excellency of dignity and the excellency of power'" (Genesis 49:3, NKJV).

In his heart, as the oldest son, Reuben thinks he is about to receive a double portion of the blessing due the eldest son, including the important task of leading the family, the priesthood, and naming of the land after him. Instead, his father declares the negative, saying, "'Unstable as water, you shall not excel'" (Genesis 49:4, NKJV). Everyone in the room gasps as Reuben's face turns ashen. The Holy Spirit speaks through Jacob, who knows Reuben lacks character and cannot lead the nation. Reuben never excels or rises to prominence; not one of the judges in Israel was a Reubenite. His would be the first tribe to be carried into captivity by the Assyrians (see 1 Chronicles 5:26).

If that weren't bad enough, Jacob adds a scathing declaration over his firstborn's unconfessed sexual sin: "'Because you went up to your father's bed; then you defiled it—he went up to my couch'" (Genesis 49:4, NKJV). 40 years earlier, Reuben had had sex with Jacob's concubine, Bilhah. There had been ample time for him to confess this grievous sin and receive forgiveness; instead, Reuben covered up his adulterous act. On a day when all things hidden are exposed, Reuben reaps what he sowed. This prophetic proclamation over Reuben is historical proof that unconfessed sins will find us out. Our loving Father is eager to forgive us all of our sins, if we are willing to confess them: "If we confess our sins, He is faithful and just to forgive us our sins and to cleanse us from all unrighteousness" (1 John 1:9, NKJV).

Simeon and Levi

Brothers Simeon and Levi step forward to the judgment seat of Jacob. Because of Reuben's verbal chastisement, they now know that this day has become a day of reckoning. Jacob declares: "'Simeon and Levi are brothers; instruments of cruelty are in their dwelling place. Let not my soul enter their council; let not my honor be united to their assembly; for in their anger they slew a man, and in their self-will they hamstrung an ox'" (Genesis 49:5-6, NKJV).

The two brothers remember their sister, Dinah, who had been raped by Shechem. Shechem loved Dinah and asked his father, Hamor, to request her hand in marriage. Hamor's family offered a dowry, friendship, and a proposal that the two peoples live in peace. Simeon and Levi deceitfully agree on one condition: all the males get circumcised. Simeon and Levi had no intentions of giving Dinah to Shechem or of living in peace with the native people, whom they plot to kill. Three days later, when the men of Shechem are in great pain, Simeon and Levi take their swords and kill every male in the city, as well as carry off their flocks, herds, other wealth, and women and children.

Just like Reuben's sin, emotionally driven actions are one of their weaknesses, with their unbridled, rage-producing murder. Jacob's prophetic statement continues: "'Cursed be their anger, for it is fierce; and their wrath, for it is cruel. I will divide them in Jacob and scatter them in Israel'" (Genesis 49:7, NKJV). This prophecy is fulfilled. Simeon's tribe would eventually be dispersed throughout Israel among the tribes of Ephraim, Manasseh, and Naphtali (2 Chronicles 34:6). When Moses comes to bless the tribes, he transforms Jacob's judgment of Levi into a blessing, but Simeon he passes over in silence (Deuteronomy 33:8-11).

However, with Levi, we see the grace of God in action. God scatters Levi and his descendants throughout Israel, just as He did Simeon's. Yet, while God judiciously scatters Levi, because of his bold stand for God while in the wilderness (Exodus 32:26), God makes Levi high priest over the nation of Israel. Think of it: Only the grace of God could take a cruel man like Levi and make him the head all the priests in Israel. God's prophetic blessing is permanent, for God decided there would always be a Levite to serve Him (Jeremiah 33:21-22).

The Tribe of Judah

Judah, Leah's fourth son, slowly takes his place before his father, waiting for his prophetic word. While waiting, I believe he frets, wondering which transgression his father will choose to display. Maybe he will say something about his pagan wife and the sons he had with her (Genesis 38:1-5), or him impregnating his daughter-in-law, Tamar (Genesis 38:11-14), during one of his out-of-town trips.

His thoughts are interrupted as Jacob speaks the first element of his blessing over his son: "'Judah, you are he whom your brothers shall praise; your hand shall be on the neck of your enemies; your father's children shall bow down before you'" (Genesis 49:8, NKJV). Judah is stunned by this prophecy; Jacob makes no mention of Judah's decadent past.

I can imagine Judah thinking, "Why no verbal parade of transgression? What did I do to avoid judgment and receive this mind-boggling prophetic blessing? Why would my father's children bow down before me?" But the Holy Spirit has revealed to Jacob the divine lineage of Judah. Jacob calls his son a "lion's whelp" and goes on to describe the coming of the Lion of the Tribe of Judah: Jesus.

This prophetic blessing is later fulfilled, as we can see in John 18:31: "Then Pilate said to them, 'You (the Jewish people, the tribe of Judah) take Him (Jesus) and judge Him according to your law'" (NKJV). Listen closely to the Jewish leaders' response: "'Therefore the Jews said to him (Pilate), 'It's not lawful for us to put anyone to death'" (NKJV). The Jewish leaders confess they had no authority to put anyone to death; by their own confession, they were under Roman authority, and Genesis 49:10 was fulfilled.

Jacob closes his prophetic utterance to Judah: "'Binding his donkey to the vine, and his donkey's colt to the choice vine, He washed his garments in wine, and his clothes in the blood of grapes. His eyes are darker than wine, and his teeth whiter than milk'" (Genesis 49:11-12, NKJV).

Who is Jacob talking about? What is the Holy Spirit showing him that will happen centuries in the future? Jesus Christ riding into Jerusalem on a donkey, soon to be offered as the Lamb of God, slain from the foundation of the world. When Jacob whispers, "He washed his clothes in wine," he is referring to blood. Christ's cleansing blood. When Jesus comes the second time, His garments will be red with blood, but this time, the blood will be from the enemies of Israel.

When Jacob sees Judah, he does not see his transgressions; they are blotted out. When Jacob's feeble eyes look on his son or his spirit, all he sees is the coming King. When Jacob sees Judah, all he can see is the Messiah, who died as a Lamb for our sins and resurrected as a lion, conquering the enemies of Israel, as well as death, hell, and the grave.

Story of Zebulun

When Leah's sixth (and youngest) son approaches the judgment seat of Jacob, he stands quietly, not knowing what to expect. Jacob pronounces his blessing: Zebulun shall dwell by the sea. His tribe shall become a haven for ships, and his borders shall adjoin Sidon.

Zebulun was to be a commercial and seafaring tribe. This prophetic blessing is fulfilled through the members of the tribe of Zebulun, whose people jeopardized their lives to the point of death (Judges 5:18) in Israel's victory over Jabin and Sisera. When Jacob says, "His border shall adjoin Sidon," which was in Phoenicia, he implies that Zebulun will take part in Phoenician commerce.

The Son, Issachar

Issachar, Leah's fifth son, takes his turn to receive Jacob's prophetic blessing. Jacob, moved by the Shekinah glory of God, speaks the following words: "'Issachar is a strong donkey lying down between two burdens; he saw that rest was good, and that the land was pleasant. He bought his shoulders to hear a burden and become a band of slaves'" (Genesis 49:14-15, NKJV).

This blessing is fulfilled too, since the tribe of Issachar will be exalted in the northern part of Israel. When Jacob looks at Issachar, he speaks of his great strength by comparing him to a strong donkey. The donkey reminds Israel they were a separated people; their trust was to be in the Lord, not in horses or chariots. The tribe of Issachar was remembered as 87,000 "mighty men of valor" (1 Chronicles 7:5), who were ready and willing to do God's bidding. Life is for one generation, but a name is forever.

Dan, Gad, Asher, and Naphtali

Jacob motions for Dan, Gad, Asher, and Naphtali to come forward. These are the sons born of the servants, Bilhah and Zilpah. In ancient Israel, it was permitted for the wife to give her husband a servant as a concubine in order to have children. This is what Sarah did in presenting Hagar to Abraham. However, to be born of a concubine was not in the same social standing as being born of a wife. When Dan, Gad, Asher, and Naphtali stood before

Jacob, they wondered if they would be included in the prophetic blessing—and they were. I perceive God shows no partiality (Acts 10:34). We are all one in Christ. We are one family with one Lord, one faith, and one baptism.

Dan

Jacob has a prophetic vision for Dan: "'Dan shall judge his people as one of the tribes of Israel. Dan shall be a serpent by the way, a viper by the path that bites the horse's heels so that its rider shall fall backward'" (Genesis 49:16-18). This comes to pass; out of this tribe comes one of the most magnificent judges in all Israel, Samson. Samson's exploits became a legend in Israel.

Yet the negative element of this vision concerns Dan being called a viper that bites the horse's heels. The tribe of Dan introduced idolatry into Israel (Judges 18:30-31). In addition, Jeroboam set up one of his golden calves in Dan (1 Kings 12:2-30). Still, the Holy Spirit reveals one last element for Dan: pardon. "'I have waited for your salvation, O Lord!'" (Genesis 49:18, NKJV).

The first reference to salvation in the Bible occurs in connection to Dan. Peering through the telescope of time, Jacob declares that the Lord's covenant for a thousand generations will bring salvation. Jacob speaks of grace in the midst of judgment, forgiveness in the midst of transgression, and redemption in the midst of deceit. Salvation, grace, forgiveness, and redemption are still available to all who ask.

Gad

Gad steps forward and Jacob's voice—though weak—is filled with God's anointing. Jacob prophesies: "'A troop shall tramp upon him, but he shall triumph at last'" (Genesis 49:19). Jacob saw Gad as conquered and yet triumphant. The tribe of Gad will be in a constant state of warfare. Still, it will have its superstars, including the prophet, Elijah. Gad was a warrior and an overcomer, a man who acted in a day when action determined the destiny of men and nations.

Asher

Asher is called to the judgment seat by Jacob. Jacob focuses on Asher like a laser beam as the Holy Spirit reveals his future. Jacob prophesies life's rewards and royal riches for this son. Bread from Asher shall be rich, and he shall yield royal dainties. This prophecy was fulfilled in 1 Kings 17:9, when Elijah was fed with bread by the widow of Zarephath. Zarephath was in Sidon, which was in Asher's territory (Joshua 19:28).

The "royal dainties" mentioned in verse 20 are later fulfilled in the scene described in Luke 2:36-38: "Now there was one, Anna, a prophetess, the daughter of Phanuel, of the tribe of Asher. She was of a great age, and had lived with a husband seven years from her virginity; and this woman was a widow of about eighty-four years, who did not depart from the temple, but served God with fasting and prayers night and day. And coming in that instant she gave thanks to the Lord, and spoke of Him to all those who looked for redemption in Jerusalem" (NKJV).

Naphtali

Jacob prophesies over the last-born son of his maidservant: "'Naphtali is a deer let loose; he uses beautiful words'" (Genesis 49:21, NKJV). The King James Version translates this verse: "'Naphtali is a hind let loose: he giveth goodly words.'" Hind describes a female deer, a timid, swift, and graceful creature of the woods. In Naphtali's early life, he apparently had been a wild, uncontrolled, yet graceful young man. Some scholars suggest when the brothers returned from Egypt with the news that Joseph was alive,

Naphtali ran ahead to tell his father that not only was all well with Benjamin, but Joseph was alive, too.

The second element of Naphtali's prophetic blessing was he uses godly words. I am sure Jacob was recalling the scene of his son gracefully, swiftly running towards him across the green pastures, bringing beautiful words about his beloved sons of Rachel. All is well with Benjamin, and Joseph is alive. As Naphtali stands before Jacob, Jacob recalls that moment of good news; in turn, Jacob expresses love to Naphtali.

Joseph

As the first-born of Jacob's beloved wife, Rachel, Joseph has always occupied a special place in his father's heart, as evidenced by the coat of many colors Jacob had given him years before. Joseph was special, too, as seen by his ascension to the number two position in Egypt despite his status as a Hebrew. Jacob starts by calling his son "a fruitful bough" whose branches "run over the wall" (Genesis 49:22), and despite attacks against him, he remained strong because of the God of Jacob.

Jacob's blessing concludes: "'By the God of your father who will help you, and by the Almighty who will bless you with blessings of heaven above, blessings of the deep that lies beneath, blessings of the breasts and of the womb. The blessings of your father have excelled the blessings of my ancestors, up to the utmost bound of the everlasting hills. They shall be on the head of Joseph, and on the crown of the head of him who was separate from his brothers'" (Genesis 49:25-26, NKJV).

One of the most magnificent prophetic overlays in Scripture involves the similarities between the life of Joseph and the life of Jesus. Only a book of supernatural origin could foreshadow such a revelation: Joseph's life is a type and a shadow of Jesus Christ to come.

Benjamin

Benjamin is the son of Joseph's old age, born in the same hour that Rachel, the love of his life, died. Jacob very lovingly places his hand over Benjamin's head and prophesies: "'Benjamin is a ravenous wolf, in the morning he shall devour his prey and at night he shall divide his spoil'" (Genesis 49:27, NKJV). The largest and fiercest of the canine family, the wolf is a relentless predator. It is the relentless and ravenous wolf Jacob foresees in the future for his youngest son. Indeed, Benjamin will become a warrior tribe in Israel.

Benjamin's descendants were fierce warriors, depicted in the story of the concubine at Gibeah (Judges 19:20). They were Israel's champion by defeating Moab, Edom, and Philistia (1 Samuel 14). Mordecai came from the tribe of Benjamin, and he and Queen Esther would defeat the dreaded Haman (Esther 8:7). Saul of Tarsus, who, after his dramatic conversion on the road to Damascus, became the mighty apostle, Paul, that possessed Benjamin's fierce and relentless warrior instinct that established the New Testament church.

Paul's farewell to the church at Ephesus in Acts 20:17-38 offers a true portrait of a Benjamin spirit. It includes these words: "I have shown you in every way, by laboring like this, that you must support the weak. And remember the words of the Lord Jesus, that He said, 'It is more blessed to give than to receive'" (NKJV).

The Priestly Blessing

The song "The Blessing," which by the summer of 2020 had become a Christian anthem recorded by more than one hundred groups, has its origins in the priestly blessing of Numbers 6:22-27: "And the Lord spoke to Moses, saying: 'Speak to Aaron and his sons, saying, "This is the way you shall bless the children of Israel. Say to them: 'The Lord bless you and keep you; the Lord make His face shine upon you, and be gracious to you; the Lord lift up His countenance upon you, and give you peace.'" So they shall put my name on the children of Israel, and I will bless them'" (NKJV).

The name Rockefeller will open the doors of finance. The name "I am Stan" (Lee) will open the doors of science. The name Beethoven will open the doors of music halls around the world. But it is only the name of the Lord that opens the doors of heaven with blessings you cannot contain. God commanded Moses to tell Aaron to read and speak aloud the transforming promises from God on the children of Israel whenever they met. The power of the prophetic blessing has changed the course of many lives and positively impacted many congregations. The priestly blessing was not just for Moses, Aaron, and elite members of the tribe of Levi. It was intended for every person on the face of the earth.

Through the priestly blessing, God is bestowing his favor on His creation. The blessing is the purest expression of His mercy and grace. God blesses his children by giving us life and provision. The priestly blessing is composed of three major promises:

1) The Lord bless you and keep you

The first sentence captures God's guarantee of abundant life for the righteous. God's blessings on His children are countless and personal. The first part of the first promise, "bless you," declares the Lord's goodness. This promise invokes the favor of God without limit, which includes physical, emotional, relational, and material abundance.

The second part of the first promise, "keep you," states that God will not only bestow His unmerited favor on you, He will also protect you and the many blessings He has imparted to you. As believers, we are not alone; we are assisted by and defended by powerful angels whom God has assigned on our behalf. God promises to guard and protect us. In turn, we keep His covenant by loving Him and keeping His commandments.

2) The Lord make His face to shine upon you and be gracious to you

The first part of the second promise, "the Lord make His face shine upon you" means to dwell in the presence of God. Believers dwell with God by abiding and dwelling in His Word. As Psalm 119:105 says, "Your word is a lamp to my feet, and a light to my path" (NKJV).

The second part of this promise, "and be gracious to you" translates in Hebrew to "show favor or to be gracious to you." There are two significant certainties within this phrase. First, man cannot demand God's presence; second, in His sovereignty, God chooses to whom He will reveal His presence. God's infinite grace is displayed in the fact that He sent His Son to dwell among us. Through Christ, God the Father reveals Himself. It is God who commanded light to shine out of darkness.

3) The Lord lift up His countenance upon you and give you peace

The third promise conveys God's approval. The Lord lifts up His countenance upon you—simply defined as "God will smile upon you." The Lord will reflect his glory through you "and give you peace."

The second part within the promise is "shalom," meaning peace. Peace in the natural is defined as the absence of war or struggle. However, in the supernatural element of the priestly blessing, shalom means to be finished or completed. In the midst of conflicting forces and circumstances, God can give us peace. The Father's peace is complete and whole, surpassing all understanding and lacking nothing. When our heavenly Father smiles on His children, it produces a sense of security, acceptance, and wholeness. More importantly, with God's peace, you can enjoy all other promises of the priestly blessing: provision, protection, wisdom, redemption, and favour.

In the final portion of the priestly blessing, the Lord instructs Aaron and his sons to invoke his name on the children of Israel, so that God Himself can sanctify Israel with the holiness that is embodied by the Name. Only then will the people be worthy of His blessing. This was the reminder that even though the priests pronounce the words of the blessing, only God can bless. The Name reveals the one true God, the One who was, is, and is to come. As 1 Corinthians 8:6 says, "Yet for us there is one God, the Father, of whom are all things, and we for Him; and one Lord Jesus Christ, through whom are all things, and through whom we live" (NKJV).

Therefore, by placing His name upon His children, God reminds us of who He is. This defines His character and what he has done, declares His mighty works, and tells of His promise, which is His covenant. This decree underscores that God and God alone is the source of all blessings in every realm of life. The scriptural reference to "blessing" has several connotations in Hebrew; when God blesses man, it is to bestow good health, abundant success, and prosperity, both materially and spiritually. When a man blesses God, it is presented in forms of thanksgiving, reverence, obedience, praise, and worship. When a man blesses His fellow believers, he recites the priestly blessing of Numbers 6:22-27 and then proclaims the Holy Spirit-inspired prophetic blessing. Such joy! Such promise! Such blessing!

CHAPTER EIGHT

Learning from the Master

Through experience, I know men and women who desire to enter into ministry—or sense God's call to ministry on their lives—must begin their journey by serving in the house of God. I served my father, who was my pastor and spiritual covering. That started with helping him build the church physically from the ground up, using bricks and sand mortar. I mixed mortar, pushed the wheelbarrow, built scaffolding, swept, and cleaned.

Once we completed the building, every Saturday afternoon I helped my wife and my mother clean up the church. Congregants from our local church lived in different suburbs. Because finding transportation to come to church posed a major challenge for many of them, I helped drive the church bus to pick up people. After the service, I dropped them off at their various homes. I helped with music and other programs of the church, too.

This experience helped me when I started my own ministry. I gave direction to children's and youth ministry and established the vision for the church. Driving people to and from church helped me to better understand people, love them, share with them, and help them with their challenges. In doing this, I became a natural "people person." Serving humbles you, adds practical knowledge to your CV, and helps you understand people. I have learned that people are the most valuable and important asset in ministry.

We are to serve like Jesus served. Although Christ was equal with God, He "emptied Himself, taking the form of a bond-servant, and being made in the likeness of men" (Philippians 2:7, NASB). In this verse, Jesus, the Son of God—who existed from the beginning and helped in creation—emptied Himself of divinity, put on humanity, and served. Look at other Scriptures, like Matthew 20:28, which says, "Just as the Son of Man did not come to be served, but to serve, and to give his life as a ransom for many" (NIV). Just prior to that, He told the disciples, "'You know that the rulers of the Gentiles lord it over them, and their high officials exercise authority over them. Not so with you. Instead, whoever wants to become great among you must be your servant'" (Matthew 20:25-27, NIV).

Through my ministerial experience, I have learned the way to greatness is to be and become a servant. My encouragement to all men and women of God who aspire to enter into ministry is to learn to serve and learn to be a servant. There are only two jobs that start from the top: well-digging and grave-digging. All the rest start from the bottom.

A Pivotal Relationship

The father-and-son relationship is so pivotal in the history of Scripture that I will devote three chapters to it. After discussing the need to become a servant in this chapter, I will review the necessity of becoming a student, and then focus on becoming a son.

The story of Elijah and Elisha shows how leadership anointing can be passed from one person to the other. Now, it's not the only case of leadership impartation in the Bible—for example, there was Moses to Joshua, and

Paul to Timothy. The pattern appears early in Scripture. Deuteronomy 34:9 says, "Now Joshua the son of Nun was full of the spirit of wisdom, for Moses had laid his hands on him; so the children of Israel heeded him, and did as the Lord had commanded Moses" (NKJV).

This same transfer is evident in 2 Kings 2:15, after Elijah had departed from the earth: "Now when the sons of the prophets who were from Jericho saw him they said, *'The spirit of Elijah rests on Elisha.'* And they came to meet him and bowed to the ground before him" (NKJV, emphasis added).

Paul and Timothy display a similar relationship, which Paul outlined in his letter to the Philippians: "But I trust in the Lord Jesus to send Timothy to you shortly, that I also may be encouraged when I know your state. For I have no one like-minded, who will sincerely care for your state. For all seek their own, not the things which are of Christ Jesus. But you know his proven character, that as a son with his father he served with me in the gospel" (Philippians 2:19-22, NKJV).

One thing to notice about God is that He doesn't start with mass production. When He created the human race, he didn't start with 1,000 people at a time or 1,000,000, (although He could have). We now have about 7.8 billion people on this planet, but God started with one man and one woman, and out of them He produced all of us. When God wanted to build the nation of Israel, He raised up Abraham, and out of Abraham came Isaac. Out of Isaac came Jacob and Esau, and out of Jacob came the 12 sons who became the 12 tribes, and so forth. God always creates a prototype and multiplies it. The same is true with leadership.

This is key with the story of Elijah, whose spirit rested on Elisha. In context, "spirit" means abilities, aptitudes, and wisdom. Aptitude is the frame of mind—the way someone looks at the world—and wisdom is the way they act. So these three key traits of the prophet rested on Elisha. This shows it is possible for a person to inherit great leadership attributes from another. It also means:

1) The spirit of a leader is transferable. Moses transferred what he had to Joshua, Elijah transferred what he had to Elisha, and Paul transferred what he had to Timothy.

2) There are processes for transferring a leader's spirit. Certain people are able to receive, while others are not. While Elisha was able to receive from Elijah, his servant Gehazi could not receive from Elisha.

3) Receiving the spirit of a leader enables us to do what they do. It's not enough to just admire a person, but that the abilities you admire are replicated in your life. I can say I admire some great leader, but what is more important is that I am able to do what they do. Leadership is not just to be admired, but also replicated. Every leader, including myself, wants to see numerous people replicating the skills and abilities they admire.

The Origin of a Relationship

The Elijah-Elisha relationship originated in 1 Kings 19:15-21, where God gave Elijah instructions on what he was to do at this point in his ministry: Go to Damascus, anoint Hazael king over Syria, Jehu king over Israel, and Elisha as a prophet in Elijah's place. The passage concludes with relating how Elisha pursued Elijah: "And he left the oxen and ran after Elijah, and said, 'Please let me kiss my father and my mother, and then I will follow you.' And he said to him, 'Go back again, for what have I done to you?' So Elisha turned back from him, and took a yoke of oxen and slaughtered them and boiled their flesh, using the oxen's equipment, and gave it to the people, and they ate. Then he arose and followed Elijah, and became his servant" (1 Kings 19:20-21, NKJV).

This passage is quite interesting. God told Elijah to anoint a prophet and the kings of Syria and Israel, even though Syria was not under Israel. This shows the prophet's ministry extended beyond his own country. In addition, if you dig deeper into the Scriptures, you will see there is no record Elijah anointed any of the three—if we interpret anointing to be the literal pouring of oil on the head or the entire body.

While God said to anoint, Elijah didn't pour oil on anyone. Instead, Elisha received the anointing through a process. If you don't understand it, you will rush out for symbols instead of substance. For many Christians, anointing oil has a largely replaced process; if you want to buy a car, you go and anoint it. Or if you plan to buy land, you pour oil on the property, as if it were a magical process that brings transference of power. Yet, although Elijah doesn't pour any oil on Elisha, a transfer takes place. A transfer that followed three key actions by Elijah:

1) He discovered Elisha

Based on God's leading, Elijah went looking for Elisha. While the Bible doesn't say they knew each other previously, it's quite possible Elisha was a student in Elijah's school of prophets. Look at the nature of the instruction; where Elisha's name is mentioned, so is his father's. So the mentor goes looking for the mentee and discovers him. When Elijah finds Elisha, he is not prophesying but ploughing. A farmer? While it may look like the wrong gift in the wrong place, it tells us that potential can be found in the unlikeliest of places. Talent isn't necessarily "on stage." People you don't think have much ability have ability; people you don't think can do much will do much.

2) He threw his mantle on Elisha

Elijah threw his mantle over Elisha. The mantle was not the spirit, but an indication of what would happen later to Elisha. The mantle was an outer garment Elisha was identified with. It is obvious when you read this passage Elijah didn't leave the mantle with Elisha that day because later, Elijah gave the mantle to him again. It's almost like Elijah used the mantle to touch Elisha but kept back the mantle because at this time, it didn't belong to Elisha. There is a temporary moment where Elisha receives an impartation that shows him what he can be in the future.

3) Elijah allowed Elisha to decide the way forward

Elijah didn't put him under pressure. Throughout their relationship, Elijah made a conscious effort to discourage Elisha. He didn't encourage him; Elijah tried to discourage him. When Elisha said, "Let me go say goodbye to my parents," he replies, "What have I done to you?" In other words, "It's up to you. I have just shown you that you could be a prophet, but it's up to you. You can decide to continue to be a farmer, you can decide to follow me, you can decide to stay, you can decide to kiss your parents… Whatever you want to do is up to you because leadership is not by force." The decision you make today will determine your future.

The anointing doesn't come by human wisdom or force; you must be ready to receive it. Many times, people have said, "I want you to train me and help me because I want to be like you." Even though it's been years since it became a worldwide box office smash, I still remember *The Karate Kid*. This kid goes to a martial arts expert—a Kung-Fu master—to learn how to fight. The old guy gives him a duster and tells him to dust one way and then the other. The kid does it for days, and he's wondering: "What does dusting have to do with martial arts? I came here to learn how to fight!"

Eventually, the master tells him he is training him how to block blows and develop ability and reflexes. Sometimes the lessons you learn to become who you want to become doesn't seem to relate to what you are looking for. And so, you start the process. You want to be a prophet; you want to be taught how to say, "Thus says the Lord," but that's not how it works.

Strength of Character

Elisha's responses are significant, too. How did he respond to this encounter with Elijah? There are six attributes that stand out from Elisha's character:

1) Elisha was a very resourceful person

Elisha was ploughing with 12 oxen, a sign of an entrepreneur. Most likely, he was in a family business and had people working for him. While he employed at least 11 other people, it is most likely he employed more. Even 12 oxen means he was ploughing a large field. He was resourceful and committed to doing something. God doesn't use lazy people to do His work. The people whom Jesus called as His disciples were already busy—balancing account books, mending nets, and fishing. They were always doing something.

I can't count how many times people have asked what they can do to become a pastor. Several have said something along the lines of: "My brother's at home and not doing anything. Can you help him to become a pastor?" Now, if he is doing nothing at home and becomes a pastor, he will do nothing at the church. People who do nothing do nothing. The Holy Spirit does not call those who are not occupied in the Lord's business.

2) Elisha was receptive

The moment the mantle touches him, the Bible says he left his oxen and ran after Elijah. The prophet didn't tell him whether to run or to stay, but Elisha was receptive to this moment of destiny. He left what he was doing to pursue Elijah. Elisha pursues the anointing and the oil, which were carriers of his grace.

3) Elisha was responsible

He sought permission from his parents to separate from the family. He worked in the family business; his parents trusted him with 12 oxen and other employees. But he doesn't just take off. He says, "Let me go settle accounts with my parents, and then I can follow you." Whenever God is shifting you from one season to another or from one place to another, it's important how you leave. If you get a new job, tell your former boss, "I've gotten a new job, and I am moving on." Don't just not appear one Monday when your old employer expects you to tackle an assignment. That's irresponsible. Most people don't know how to exit. Exiting with integrity carries a blessing. Don't burn the bridge behind you because some day you will need it to cross over.

4) Elisha was resolute

He killed his oxen and burned the equipment. In other words, he made sure he was through with this farming. He wasn't going to farm again because he was responding to this call. He was determined and resolute. When I left my secular employment, I was a plan-drawer. I gave all my drawing equipment to fellow friends at work—making a decision I was not going to come back.

5) Elisha readjusted

He fed people with the meat of his oxen, demonstrating that from now on, he wouldn't work to feed himself; he would readjust his focus to feeding other people. He was going to work to make other people's lives better.

6) Elisha was respectful

He followed Elijah and became his servant. He moved from being the boss of his farm workers to becoming Elijah's servant. Now, if you were observing this, you would say the guy had stepped down. Eleven people looked up to him, and he had his own business . . . why would he lower himself? I can just picture the people asking him, "Are you in your right mind? Look at all that you have! Look at all that you have achieved! Why are you going to be somebody's small boy?"

There will always be people who will criticize certain moves you make and make you feel as if you have lost your brain. But that is the unique thing about Elisha, because if there is going to be a transference, the first thing that starts it is possessing the spirit of a servant. Not the spirit of a *master*, but the spirit of a *servant*. When I left my secular job, my family, friends, and boss thought I was crazy. My boss told me ministry was for lazy folks. But today, those who thought I was crazy are at the same place they were while I took the step of faith, and God blessed me a hundredfold.

The Servanthood Nature

What does it mean that Elisha became his servant? There are several key lessons here:

1) He surrendered his own agenda. Many who seek the mantle of leadership never surrender their own agenda. They stay around the person they want to receive from while always looking for an occasion to advance their own interests. Gehazi was a clear example, as was Judas.

2) He submitted himself to Elijah. It was a willing choice, not one demanded from him. In the process of becoming a leader, there will always be a time of submission or surrender. One reason it's difficult in

certain cultures to follow a progressive path to leadership is because the people don't understand what it means to serve.

3) He shouldered Elijah's burden. He made it easier for Elijah to do his work by doing for Elijah what he couldn't do for himself or was weighing him down.

4) He supported Elijah's vision and interests. He sided with Elijah, so the prophet's battles became Elisha's, and his enemies became Elisha's enemies. You cannot be on a different side than your master. I have observed working in different places and cultures that if you go to an advancing economy and pick a shop assistant to talk with about where they work, you'll be amazed by the enthusiasm with which they speak! They praise the organization and its vision and speak highly of their products, insisting they are better than their competitors. They speak highly of their bosses.

But in most environments, when you ask someone their opinion of where they work, it touches off a litany of complaints. Sometimes they undermine their own products and organization while speaking against the boss and co-workers. I think it's one of the reasons it is difficult to pass on success stories from one generation to the next in various parts of the world—the undermining mindset with which people work. Not so with Elisha. He pursued Elijah's interests despite opportunities to turn against him, criticize him, and fight him. Elisha never did. He had set his mind on receiving a double portion. He wanted to be greater than the previous generation. If this generation wants to be greater than the previous generation, it demands a different attitude. You cannot benefit from something you disrespect.

How many of us can say: *"This is where I work, and I'm just happy, and I speak well of my place of work"*? Any time a leader finds people whose hearts are joined to his vision, it's easy for whatever he or she carries to be transferred to those people. Elisha obviously supported Elijah's interests. He didn't have a different opinion than Elijah's.

So how was he a servant? While the Bible doesn't say much about this, 2 Kings 3:11 provides an indication. This is when Israel was in trouble; it expected an attack from Moab. They were looking for a prophet, but Elijah was long gone, and Elisha wasn't on the scene: "But Jehoshaphat said, 'Is there no prophet of the Lord here, that we may inquire of the Lord by him?' So one of the servants of the king of Israel answered and said, 'Elisha the son of Shaphat is here, *who poured water on the hands of Elijah*'" (NKJV, emphasis added).

The final words of the verse reveal how Elisha served. He focused on Elijah and not on his gift. He washed Elijah's hands, not his own. If you study this story, you will see Elisha didn't go in first to learn how to prophesy. He went in to meet physical needs—wash Elijah's things, his clothes, his hands. In our part of the world, people would say, "Iron his clothes and do 'menial' jobs like polishing his shoes?" And many would ask, "Why are you polishing shoes? What does that have to do with prophecy?"

Stepping into Greatness

For Elisha, serving had everything to do with his prophetic anointing. His step toward greatness started with servanthood. It reflects what Jesus taught in Matthew 20:25-26: "But Jesus called them to Himself and said, 'You know that the rulers of the Gentiles lord it over them, and those who are great exercise authority over them. Yet it shall not be so among you; but whoever desires to become great among you, let him be your servant'" (NKJV).

How many of you want to be great? The Lord didn't say, "If you want to be great, go and print a card with your name and titles on it." He didn't say, "If you want to be great, go and sell yourself." In modern times, many emphasize the need to "market yourself." What that translates to is speaking more highly of yourself than you ought, a direct contradiction of Romans 12:3: "For I say, through the grace given to me, to everyone who is among you, not to think of himself more highly than he ought" (NKJV).

Have you read the kind of CVs or resumes people put out these days? They say "I am" able to do enterprise, "I am" a good team player, and "I'm this" and "I'm that." The question is: If you are all of this, why are you that? Don't you think if you were as good as this paper says you are, you wouldn't be sitting in front of me looking for this job? You would be the greatest thing since chocolate. Everybody would be out there looking for you! But Jesus says, "If you are going to be great, don't promote yourself. Instead, be a servant." This is what Elisha understood: The way to greatness is through servanthood. The way up is down. Can you imagine the kind of work environments we would enjoy and the kind of people we would produce if young men and women became Elishas and entered the workforce with his attitude?

In Luke 16:12, Jesus says, "'And if you have not been faithful in what is another man's, who will give you what is your own?'" (NKJV). Those words emphasize two key concepts: 1) servanthood is the path to greatness and 2) stewardship is the key to ownership. If you have not faithfully stewarded someone else's property, business, or enterprise, who will give you your own? The path to leadership is impartation, which starts with being a servant.

This concept is vital when you consider what Elisha received: a double portion of what Elijah had. In other words, Elisha became greater than his master—greater in terms of the volume of his work and activity. But he didn't start by just desiring greatness, he started by serving. I know young men and women are hungry for success. While that is good, if you are going to be great, first you must serve. It's the path to the double portion.

Exalted Role

To return to the sad story of that ministerial dropout, I don't think he saw the role of John the Baptist as that exalted—certainly not in comparison to Jesus. But John the Baptist was quite necessary in preparing the way for Christ. Jesus based His ministry on what John accomplished. So for anyone reading these words who is high-minded and think you are going to be greater than everyone who came before you, remember: If you want to be the Elisha who gets a double portion of Elijah's spirit, you must start where Elisha started: with being a servant.

You've got to serve somebody and pour water on their hands. You will have to learn, throw away your own ambitions, kill your oxen and distribute their flesh, burn your implements, and then submit to an Elijah. Tell this person: "I've done so much by myself, but I want to do far more. And you are the key to the far more, so I choose to serve under you." That is the beginning of greatness! You do it with sincerity, integrity, and respect, without complaining and by shouldering the burden. And over time, the double portion will rest upon you.

CHAPTER NINE

The Teachable Spirit

Many of you are in places where God has brought people into your life, but you have no idea what kind of value they will add to you. Don't be like me, having to look back 40 years later at missed opportunities from my youth and sighing the sigh of lament: "I missed my opportunity." If you are going to be a great leader, you must understand the significant moments in life. The places you go to, people you meet, and situations God puts you into are learning opportunities that you need to grasp. Your future depends on it.

Imitating a Leader

Every great leader begins his journey by following somebody and imitating a process. To follow is to go where another person is going. When you are following, you don't determine where you want to go, you go where the leader takes you. When Elisha followed Elijah, the implication was he would walk behind Elijah, imitate him, and go where the prophet was going. The process of leadership development requires followership, so you can rise one day to become a leader. Every leader is a follower, and followers can become leaders. Nigerian writer and poet Bamigboye Olurotimi counsels: "Don't waste your time following a man for following sake, follow him because he has a large heart to lift you up and lead you on the path of discovery, purposeful living, success, and accomplishments."[6]

The Lord Jesus taught the principle of followership, which can be seen through two passages. The first is Matthew 4:19-20. Jesus called His disciples, and the Bible says, "He said to them, 'Follow me, and I will make you fishers of men.' They immediately left their nets and followed him" (NKJV). Jesus required His disciples to not just walk with Him or stay by His side. They were to imitate Him and walk in His footsteps.

Then, in Luke 6:40, He teaches a quality of followers: "'A disciple is not above his teacher, but everyone who is perfectly trained will be like his teacher'" (NKJV). In other words, there are people who are perfectly trained and people who are not. To become like the teacher, you must be perfectly trained. This requires developing the tools of a student—a follower, a disciple.

Keys for a Student

Learning from a teacher in order to become greater than that person requires five key qualities:

1) Appreciation: Value the opportunity you have. This is where everything begins. Many fail to appreciate the opportunities they have to learn from someone who is more accomplished. If someone who has done more than they agreed to teach you, they are adding value to your life. Don't take that for granted; you have significant lessons to learn. If somebody says, "I will spend a week with you and teach you a couple things," appreciate that. The impartation of wisdom is priceless.

2) Submission: A servant is not above his master. Humble yourself. You cannot be arrogant and learn. You cannot see yourself as better than your teacher and learn from him or her, so check your pride at the door. You must come in as a child, ready to learn, humble, and submissive. As a leader, I have often

tried to help people; at some point, every leader's greatest desire is to replicate themselves and multiply their influence. But sometimes people don't appreciate this opportunity. If you think you already know something, you can never receive insights.

3) Observation: Watch what is going on. Keep your eyes and senses alert, keep your heart open, and pay attention. Notice all the little things that make a difference. People can be around for a long time and never pay attention because their mind is set on what they think is important. If you never pay attention, you never learn. Observe the habits of your teacher and their priorities, values, and instructions. Two situations may look alike on the surface, but yet be very different.

4) Comprehension: Grasp what is taught. A student must be a questioner. You don't question for the purpose of challenging your teacher but to receive clarity. After many a sermon, someone has said, "Oh, pastor, I like what you preached so much!" But by the time they express what they thought I was saying, I'm depressed—it often is the exact opposite of what I said. Understanding is vital to learning. The worst thing a follower can do is wrongly interpret a lesson and assume they understand it.

5) Application: Put your lessons into practice. A disciple is a doer. Don't just master the information of the theory, implement it in your life. The only way to know whether a student has learned a lesson is to test them, which is what we see in the life of Elisha.

One quality the disciples learned from Jesus was the art of asking questions if they didn't understand something. One example appears in Matthew 16:5-12, after Jesus feeds the five thousand and then warns them to be aware of the leaven of the Pharisees and Sadducees. This touches off a great discussion amongst the disciples, who fail to understand what the Lord is warning them about. After, He explains it in detail: "Then they understood that He did not tell them to beware of the leaven of bread, *but of the doctrine of the Pharisees and Sadducees*" (Matthew 16:12, NKJV, emphasis added).

Leaven is yeast, which is used to make bread. Jesus was warning against accepting even a tiny bit of the Pharisees' or Sadducees' teaching, since ingesting mistaken doctrine would rise in their spirit like yeast in a loaf of bread. Finally, they understood: "Oh! He means their doctrine." This shows how people will often interpret things based on their own experience. But when you are following a leader, your experience is not the most important factor—it is the knowledge the leader is imparting. The disciples were trying to bring Christ's statement down to their level of experience. If you are going to be a great student, comprehension matters. If you don't understand, seek clarification rather than making assumptions.

Important Lessons

Elisha followed Elijah for eight years. During this journey, there are statements Elijah makes, Elisha makes, and the sons of the prophets make. These statements are repeated by all three at every place: Gilgal, Bethel, Jericho, and Jordan. If something is repeated over and over again, it means that the repetition is to reinforce something you must not forget. Three important voices that we hear in the Scripture:

1) Elijah's voice. This is the voice of testing.

Every teacher tests his student, no matter how much the student may learn. It is examination that will determine your future, not your study. Examination will determine who gets promoted, who repeats the lesson, and who will be dismissed. So remember, if you are entering into leadership, you will be tested. It's not about how much you learn but how well you pass the test.

At this point, Elijah affirmed his mission from God. Indirectly, he was saying to Elisha, "God has called me to go to Jericho, and you are not part of this journey. So you stay." Can you imagine how embarrassed Elisha would have felt after serving Elijah and following him for this long, only to be told he's not a part of the vision? To be told he has no fatherly inheritance and cannot go to the next level? Elijah was putting Elisha's passion, loyalty, and commitment to the test. Every follower will be tested this way. Thank God Elisha passed.

2) The voice of the sons of the prophets. This is the voice of taunting.

Taunting means mocking. The reason the sons of the prophets were mocking Elisha is because they were competitors. Competitors will always mock you. The sons of the prophets were still in the school of training and hoped to be in Elisha's place. Since they weren't chosen, they taunted Elisha. Remember that those who taunt you will make a fool of your loyalty, try to discredit your call, and laugh at your servanthood. As sons of the prophets, I believe they knew Elijah was about to be taken into heaven, and once that happened, Elisha would be promoted. So instead of encouraging him, they taunted him.

It's dangerous to have prophetic knowledge and use it to mock and scare people away from their calling. As you serve your way into greatness, there will be people who will make you feel that you are foolish in doing what you are doing; they want you to give up and quit. They will say things like: "You have been serving this man for so long; what do you have? Look where you are. You are not paid enough; you don't even have a car" and other such statements. They will do anything to distract you from your God-given purpose. The sons of the prophets tried to make Elisha feel there was no future for him by pointing to a fruitless future in ministry.

A test always comes before promotion. Look at the test Elisha was facing; Elijah said to him, "Don't follow me. The sons of the prophets say you are wasting your time following me." Elijah taunted him just like the sons of the prophets.

3) The other voice of Elijah is a voice of trust.

It's trust that will hold a mentor and mentee together. It was trust that caused Elisha to tie his mission to Elijah's. Elisha said, "Wherever God calls you and God leads you, I will follow. Until this time, I have had no mission from God because He has not called me. In fact, God wants me to follow and not lead. The moment of the decision will come after I pass my test."

Elisha also said to Elijah, "As long as my soul lives and as long as your soul lives, I am stuck to you, and I am following you. I know what you have: the 'Anointing.' I am pursuing the anointing; my destiny is tied to your destiny. I may not know where you are going but following you makes me feel safe. I have direction."

Don't create a path for yourself if you don't know where you are going. If you have no direction, you might take the wrong path. Follow somebody who knows the way, and as you follow, you will create your own path. When you know your destiny is tied to something or someone, you must refuse every obstacle that comes your way and refuse to be hurt or disappointed. Elisha teaches us some profound lessons that you can stay with the voice of trust.

Lessons of Significance

Each of the four places where Elijah and Elisha stopped during their journey contains significant lessons because of the encounters that took place there. They include Gilgal, Bethel, Jericho, and Jordan.

To start with Gilgal, the name means "rolling away"—a change or transformation. The first significant biblical encounter is in Joshua: "Then Joshua circumcised their sons whom He raised up in their place; for they were uncircumcised, because they had not been circumcised on the way. So it was, when they had finished circumcising all the people, that they stayed in their places in the camp till they were healed. Then the Lord said to Joshua, 'This day I have rolled away the reproach of Egypt from you.' Therefore the name of the place is called Gilgal to this day" (Joshua 5:7-9, NKJV).

The reason it is called Gilgal is because of what happened in the days of Joshua. This is the lesson Elijah is teaching Elisha. Gilgal is a place for three important things. If you don't master them, you can never move on to the next level of leadership development:

1) The first thing that Gilgal represents is breaking with the past

At Gilgal, the children of Israel who were born in the desert had to undergo change. After all the years in the desert, they had not been circumcised, even though God gave the decree of circumcision to Abraham: On the eighth day, every male child shall be circumcised. They go into captivity, and when they leave Egypt, Moses brings them out but doesn't circumcise them. Now Moses is dead, and Joshua is the leader—40 years later! While Moses allowed the lack of circumcision to continue, Joshua did not. Sometimes there may be mistakes in our lives that one leader tolerates, but another won't.

If you are going to grow into the leader you are supposed to be, you cannot just say, "Well, when I followed Moses, he allowed it." If you are going to go to the promised land, you have to do what Joshua says; you need to come under a leader who will not tolerate mistakes. This is what they had to understand at Gilgal. Elisha had to come to that turning point in his walk with Elijah. Maybe your father tolerated something, and your mother did, too, but that bad habit is killing you. Deficiencies can get passed on in families. Dysfunctional families are where lessons are never learned or wrong things are taught. You can observe a family wrought by emotion and conflict, or one where everybody divorces. The latter isn't a curse as much as a learning process. Somebody passed on the wrong lessons from generation to generation.

Gilgal is a place where somebody comes into your life and says, "I will not tolerate the 'rubbish' from you any longer." You were lazy, and your boss tolerated it. You didn't perform, and they tolerated it. You were absent regularly from the office, and they tolerated it. But the new leader says, "It may have been okay before, but the journey ends now! This is Gilgal."

2) The second lesson about Gilgal is you must allow yourself to be corrected

At Gilgal, Joshua had to circumcise a whole generation of people. They should have been circumcised when they were eight days old, and now some of them are 40 years old. It's a very painful correction when you have been in the wrong for so long. Circumcision normally is uncomfortable, but when it happens to little children, it's fine. A child eight to 15-days-old goes to the hospital and he doesn't even know what's happening. Granted, the child cries, but the doctor puts something in his mouth, dresses the wound, and after a couple days, he is fine. But take a 40-year-old man and say, "Hey, sir, you should have gone through this when you were eight days old, but your parents didn't train you well"—now we're talking pain!

The Bible says they couldn't do anything for many days. When people correct a long-standing mistake, it hurts. You will cry adult-sized tears. You'll say, "Nobody has ever done this. Nobody has ever told me that. Nobody has ever said that I'm lazy!" You've been lazy for 40 years, but nobody has had the courage to tell you until you reach Gilgal. Your old boss may have accepted your lackadaisical efforts, but now Joshua is taking you to a better place. You must circumcise that laziness out of your life, even though it would have been better to learn that at a young age.

When our children were growing up and they wanted to touch a fire, my wife would tell them, "Hey! Don't touch that fire!" She always protected them. But I would say, "Don't protect them; let them touch it. Let the fire burn them!" I reasoned it was better to be burned by fire at six to 12 months of age and know that's something they don't want to do than to wait until they're 50 and have never been burned by fire. Yet some people don't learn lessons while they're young, whether that is table manners, proper dress, or how to talk. Then they attend a major business conference, and everyone is looking funny at them because they're eating with the wrong cutlery and talking with their mouth full. Their sloppy eating habits may cost them business contracts.

What Elijah is telling Elisha is: "If there is a mistake that must be corrected, I will not tolerate it in your life. I am going to make sure that you are purged of every liability so that you can move on to the next phase of your life." The best training may not come from your classroom or even your home. Sometimes it comes from somebody whom you meet later in life when you are full grown. That may be the person in your life who can help you become the person God has called you to be.

3) Gilgal is a place for embracing a new identity

At Gilgal, God rolled away the reproach of Egypt from the "wilderness generation." They were no longer products of Egyptian society; they were now in covenant relationship with God. The reproach of the past had been cut off. The thing that made them repeat the same mistake had been rolled away.

Sometimes people come to me and say, "I want you to mentor me; I want you to train me." Many don't appreciate what they are asking. I am not going to put my arm around you and say, "Oh, you're a good boy (or girl) and are doing well." I will Gilgal you! By the time I am through with you, you may hate me with every fiber in your being because I am going to make you undo, redo, and change. Asking for a mentor is not just adding another level to your promotional record; it is asking for circumcision. Ouch.

Encountering God

From Gilgal, they went to Bethel, which is the house of God. Elijah was not the first person to go to Bethel; this was where Abraham met God: "Then the Lordappeared to Abram and said, 'To your descendants I will give this land.' And there he built an altar to the Lord, who had appeared to him. And he moved from there to the mountain east of Bethel, and he pitched his tent with Bethel on the west and Ai on the east; there he built an altar to the Lord and called on the name of the Lord. So Abram journeyed, going on still toward the South" (Genesis 12:7-9, NKJV).

Abraham received a revelation from God at Bethel and built an altar. His grandson, Jacob, also went to Bethel when he was fleeing from Esau. Genesis 28:16-19 says, "Then Jacob awoke from his sleep and said, 'Surely the Lord is in this place, and I did not know it.' And he was afraid and said, 'How awesome is this place! This is none other than the house of God, and this is the gate of heaven!' Then Jacob rose early in the morning, and took the stone that he had put at his head, set it up as a pillar, and poured oil on top of it. And he called the name of that place Bethel; but the name of that city had been Luz previously" (NKJV).

What does Bethel stand for? Three things, starting with the fact it is a place for encountering the God of your father—your spiritual father or mentor. Abraham was the first to encounter God at Bethel, before Jacob. When God appeared to Jacob in Bethel, he said to him (in so many words), "I am the God of Abraham your father. You have made connection with the deep beliefs and the values of your mentor." Elijah knew the God of Abraham. Bethel is a place of historical encounter and historical faith. Elisha had to encounter what his father Elijah had encountered.

It's one thing to follow somebody, but quite another to get in touch with the thing that makes them who they are—namely, their core beliefs and foundation. You can be around a person for a long time and not know what makes them tick. Sometimes even your own children may never get in touch with your core beliefs. But at Bethel, Jacob encountered the God of Abraham. At Bethel, Elisha encountered the God of Elijah. Bethel is the house of God, a place of spiritual encounter and a place for receiving revelation about where you are. Jacob slept in Bethel and did not grasp its significance. That's why he said the Lord was in that place, but he didn't realize it. The symbolism is clear: Sometimes you can be in a place that is awesome and not know it.

Has it ever happened to you where you go through life, go through an experience, or meet somebody, and then years later you look back and say, "If I had known I would be here now, I would have taken this seriously years ago?" Or have you met somebody whom you knew earlier and say, "Well I met this person 15 years ago. If I had known he would be so strategic to my destiny, I would have been nicer to him then"? Jacob is saying the Lord was in this place and he didn't know it.

Sometimes the lessons of today may not seem important until years later. You fight the process and years later, you realize you should have paid attention when your instructor taught you how to write a report. You should have paid attention to topics like using the right language, sentence structure, and punctuation, like where to put a full stop. I can recognize when someone hasn't learned the basics; they write something with no commas. It runs on for so long I can't catch my breath. I can imagine them years earlier saying, "Punctuation, colon, semi-colon, comma, full stop, exclamation mark...Ah! What do I need this for?" Well, for starters, to write a coherent report.

A Place of Covenant

Bethel is also a place for making a personal covenant with God. At Bethel, both Abraham and Jacob built altars. An altar is a mark of remembrance of a spiritual experience. It identifies key moments in your life. On a recent visit, someone asked me, "So what shaped your life? What are the important things that made you who you are?" I can pinpoint those moments of transition in my life when everything changed. They are my personal altars, times when I vowed to myself that I would do or not do certain things. The reason to build altars in your life is so you never forget key lessons. The greatest disaster in your life is to make the same mistake repeatedly and never learn anything because you didn't build any altars.

If you're going to make progress in your journey to receive a double portion and a greater impartation, you are also going to go through your own Gilgal and your own Bethel. Don't be upset when you must go through these lessons. Hebrews 12:11 says, "Now no chastening seems to be joyful for the present, but painful; nevertheless, afterward it yields the peaceable fruit of righteousness to those who have been trained by it" (NKJV). The truth is, the leader who doesn't correct you doesn't like you. The Bible says whom God loves, He corrects.

It may seem like the one who let you get away with things or helped you break the rules was the right kind of leader. That is, until you realize rules matter, and breaking rules has become part of your second nature. Then you realize that person wasn't really helping you. That father or mother didn't help you because they didn't circumcise you. If that is the case, thank God for the new Joshua that is coming into your life! If you allow him, he will help you arrest past mistakes and roll away the reproach.

Dark and Light

The next place Elijah must visit is Jericho, a name that means city of the moon, a fragrant place, or a city of palm trees. It's quite interesting because Jericho can be a dark place for you or a beautiful one. It can be a place of darkness where only the moon offers light, or it can be a place of fragrance. We have to choose what Jericho will symbolize in our life. Why does Elijah take Elisha to Jericho, and what does it symbolize? We can learn from several key Scriptures:

Joshua 5:13-15: "Now when Joshua was near Jericho, he looked up and saw a man standing in front of him with a drawn sword in his hand. Joshua went up to him and asked, 'Are you for us or for our enemies?' 'Neither' he replied, 'but as commander of the army of the Lord I have now come.' Then Joshua fell facedown to the ground in reverence, and asked him, 'What message does my Lord have for his servant?' The commander of the Lord's army replied, 'Take off your sandals, for the place where you are standing is holy.' And Joshua did so" (NKJV).

Joshua 6:18-19: "But keep away from the devoted things, so that you will not bring about your own destruction by taking any of them. Otherwise you

will make the camp of Israel liable to destruction and bring trouble on it. All the silver and gold and the articles of bronze and iron are sacred to the Lord and must go into his treasury" (NKJV).
Joshua 6:3-5: *"March around the city once with all the armed men. Do this for six days. Have seven priests carry trumpets of rams' horns in front of the ark. On the seventh day, march around the city seven times, with the priests blowing the trumpets. When you hear them sound a long blast on the trumpets, have the whole army give a loud shout; then the wall of the city will collapse and the army will go up, everyone straight in" (NKJV).*

The things about Jericho that were so special start with the fact that Jericho was a place of learning—of compliance with directives and instructions. One lesson in the story of the city's fall is the detailed instructions God gave to Joshua concerning Jericho; it is not a place to do as you please but a place to do as you are directed. A student who is perfectly trained is one who pays attention to directives.

Many times in life, people fail because they do not read the instructions. Even in the examination room, some students fail to read the instructions before taking the test. Jericho is a place where you must pay attention to details, comply with instructions, and keep your eyes fixed on the right thing. Many students fail because they don't pay attention to details.

God instructed Joshua to march around the city six times silently and on the seventh day to march seven times. On the seventh time, seven priests were to hold rams' horns as they went ahead of the Ark of the Covenant. They were to blow the horn for a long time, and then the people were to shout with a great shout, and the wall would fall. If the people ignored just one of these instructions, the walls would not fall.

This is an important principle. Too many people bend God's rules to suit their lifestyle or modify the instructions they receive. Jericho is not a place to bend the rules but to master them. We all know people who never take instructions; because they always break the rules, they never succeed. You cannot get a double portion anointing if you don't pay attention and always break rules.

The second thing about Jericho is learning to know what is sacred and special. One of the instructions that God gave to Joshua was that all of the spoils—all the silver and gold—belonged to the Lord. All the precious metals were to be dedicated wholly to God. His instructions could be paraphrased: "Don't take it for yourselves; if you do, it will become an accursed thing!" Jericho is a place where you learn what is sacred and what is profane. Unfortunately, the children of Israel didn't learn these lessons and took what was not theirs.

Now, the next city they were to conquer was Ai, where God told them they could take all the gold, silver, and spoils. This applies to us today. There are some things that are not for taking if they aren't yours. Elijah was teaching Elisha a great lesson: You might be a prophet, but you don't take what's not yours. You may have all the power, but you don't have access to it.

Finally, Jericho is a place where you engage in strategic warfare. When Elijah takes Elisha to Jericho (the first city where they fought), he says to Elisha that there will be some battles he needs to know how to fight spiritually and naturally; be strategic.

Crossing Boundaries

The next place they go to is Jordan, whose name means a fast-flowing river. The Jordan runs downstream. The symbolic meaning: The river can be a barrier or a carrier. The Jordan represented the idea that it will either stop you or move you along. Ironically, the thing that stops you can be the same thing that moves you. What we can learn from the Jordan can be seen through two key Scriptures:

Joshua 1:1-3: "After the death of Moses the servant of the Lord, it came to pass that the Lord spoke to Joshua the son of Nun, Moses' assistant, saying: 'Moses My servant is dead. Now therefore, arise, go over this Jordan, you and all this people, to the land which I am giving to them—the children of Israel. Every place that the sole of your foot will tread upon I have given you, as I said to Moses'" (NKJV).

Joshua 3:14-17: "So it was, when the people set out from their camp to cross over the Jordan, with the priests bearing the ark of the covenant before the people, and as those who bore the ark came to the Jordan, and the feet of the priests who bore the ark dipped in the edge of the water (for the Jordan over-flows all its banks during the whole time of harvest), that the waters which came down from upstream stood still, and rose in a heap very far away at Adam, the city that is beside Zaretan. So the waters that went down into the Sea of the Arabah, the Salt Sea, failed, and were cut off; and the people crossed over opposite Jericho. Then the priests who bore the ark of the covenant of the Lord stood firm on dry ground in the midst of the Jordan; and all Israel crossed over on dry ground, until all the people had crossed completely over the Jordan" (NKJV).

Among the other lessons the River Jordan represents is learning to break historical limitations—in other words, limits that have been there for a long time. The same thing that limited the children of Israel limited their grandfather and other family members. Until now, no one had been able to break its back. For 40 years, the Jordan stood between them and the promised land. They knew that their inheritance was on the other side, but they could not break through this limit, which was spiritual, physical, and mental. Moses never crossed the Jordan, but Joshua did twice—the first time as an intelligence officer and the second when he led God's people across.

Moses performed many miracles, including crossing the Red Sea. Though profound in his leadership, he could never cross the Jordan. Imagine the barriers this posed for the children of Israel: "If Moses couldn't cross this, then we cannot either." We cannot let the same happen to us today. Moving into greater leadership or sonship means we need to break historical barriers. We must break down and overcome anything that has denied our inheritance and blessings.

People cannot be successful in life if they peg their life to somebody else's underperformance. If somebody was great but could not do something, it just means that the upcoming generation can do 10 times more. We must have Joshua's spirit and go where Moses never advanced. We must have Elisha's spirit and go where Elijah never went. It was at the Jordan where a new generation of sons (or leadership) emerged to break through Moses's limitations. I believe Elijah said to Elisha, "You will go where I have not been. You will break barriers and limitations that I did not break. You will achieve things that I have not achieved."

Just as Joshua led the children of Israel across Jordan, Elisha broke barriers. If you embrace this kind of faith, you, too, will do great and miraculous works that will astound your community and break every limitation. My greatest desire is to raise sons and daughters who will do far more than I have done.

Jordan also represents learning to use your mantle in new ways. At the Jordan River, Elijah took his mantle to strike the water, and the waters parted for them. Elijah took the mantle (meaning his ability, anointing, grace, skill, and competence) from his shoulder and struck the river. Until that time, people didn't think the mantle of a prophet could open a river, but Elijah was demonstrating to Elisha that there are things in your life you carry that will enable you to do far more than people expect. Sometimes people think that you can only preach and prophesy, but Elijah shows how you can also open rivers.

Don't allow people to limit what you are carrying or what you can do. Some might say to you, "This is how far you can go in life," but I am proclaiming you can go further and more. You might be a carpenter, but God has called you for more. You can grow into greatness in other areas of your life. Don't let people box you in. You have a greater ability than you can think. Who says a carpenter cannot own a law firm? You may not have the required degrees, but if this is your dream, you can employ a lawyer and pay him for achieving your dream.

Elijah was telling Elisha: "A few hours from now when this mantle drops on you, don't limit its usage, because you can open rivers with it; don't allow people to limit you." The effect of your ability is being able to extend yourself into areas that people think is not in your domain. Jordan teaches us to learn to demand greater and more. Remember only after they crossed the Jordan did Elijah ask Elisha, "What do you want from me?" Elijah finally says to Elisha, "Ask and it will be given to you." This is a powerful statement. Elisha responds by saying, "Please give me a double portion of what you have."

Elisha didn't ask for something small because he broke every limitation. In asking for a double portion, Elisha demonstrated humility and boldness. There are some who are arrogant and unappreciative, yet there are also people who are humble and gracious. You can give the latter anything they want. Elisha had the rare combination of humility and ambition. In other words, Elisha was saying, "Please, sir, I want double. I want to do more. If it pleases you, I want to be greater than you." Elisha had a big spiritual appetite but stayed humble in the process.

When Elisha said he wanted a double portion, Elijah said, "You are asking a hard thing." What Elijah really meant was, "I was not expecting you to ask me this. I thought you would ask me for something small." Elisha could only answer in this manner because he passed the test. Unfortunately, many people fail the test inherent in getting a double portion because they ask before passing the test. Without being asked what they want, many leaders stake their claim. They try to take the pulpit before being asked; they want to leave before being asked. Never stake a claim before being asked. Wait your turn, wait your moment, and when you are asked, reply with humility and boldness.

For Elisha to receive a double portion, it required eight years of serving and doing; he had to follow the process from Gilgal to Bethel, from Bethel to Jericho, and from Jericho to Jordan. Process shapes you, defines you, and brings you to your place of destiny.

CHAPTER TEN

Transfer to the Son

One of the most remarkable ministry transitions we have seen in modern times involves the founding pastor of Lakewood Church, John Osteen, and his son and current pastor, Joel Osteen. Under Joel's leadership, the Houston, Texas-based congregation has become the largest in the United States. Before the pandemic shut down in-person worship services everywhere in March of 2020, Lakewood was averaging more than 50,000 attendees per week.

Not everyone is familiar with the story of this church, which John founded in an old feed store in 1959. It eventually grew into a megachurch of more than 15,000. His weekly program aired on numerous Christian TV stations, with his straightforward, Bible-based messages helping spread his popularity across the region and eventually the nation. He also preached about faith and supernatural healing—the latter grounded in the healing of his daughter, Lisa. She was born with such severe health issues doctors said she would never experience full physical or mental capabilities. Yet she did.

Later, John's wife, Dodie, would be miraculously healed of cancer. In her autobiography, *Healed of Cancer*, she wrote, "The Word of God is extremely important to people who are fighting a battle for their health, for often it's the only hope they have. I know I would have died if it had not been for the Bible. Day by day, I gained encouragement from the precious promises that God revealed to me through His Word. I clung to my Bible and its healing promises."[7]

When John passed from this world in 1999, few imagined the church would more than triple in size under his son's leadership. After all, the elder Osteen had written more than 50 books and edited two magazines. He also held preaching revivals across the world and became a popular speaker at Full Gospel Business Men's Fellowship International meetings after getting acquainted with FBMFI's founder, Demos Shakarian, at a conference in California.

Today, Joel Osteen is more recognizable than his father in his day. Joel's first book, *Your Best Life Now*, became a *New York Times* bestseller and has surpassed sales of 100 million. By the fall of 2020, he had written 14 books in total. His church meets in the former Compaq Center, once home to the National Basketball Association's Houston Rockets. On Palm Sunday of 2020, five million viewers tuned in to his streaming service online.

The interesting aspect of this story is that for a long time, Joel was not the one being groomed to take his father's place. In 1982, Joel left Oral Roberts University to help his father start his television ministry. The outreach received a boost from John's friendship with evangelist Oral Roberts, whose producers helped establish Lakewood's presence in local, national, and international TV markets. All the while, Joel was learning; he was the student. He was in the TV room behind the camera, studying and learning.

His efforts to teach people about the goodness of God instead of feeling that He is mad at them and laboring under feelings of guilt have proved popular. In a spring 2020 interview, he told a national magazine his spiritual mission was to bring good into the world and "to lift people up, to give them hope, to help them forgive, and to help them feel better about themselves. My mission is to help them know who God is, and to know who *they* are. A lot of people, we don't know who we are. We think we're just average. I believe we are all made in the image of God, and that we have greatness in us. So, it's to lift people up and help them push into their destiny."[8]

I won't go into further detail about Joel, who has been the subject of numerous TV interviews, profiles, and articles. My point here is that John had a biological son who also became a spiritual son. This is a treasure so profound and so anointed that many fail to appreciate what God has done in Houston (and beyond) over the past six decades. We don't know whether we will see this kind of transition occur very often again before the Lord returns.

A Powerful Process

As the story of John and Joel Osteen illustrates, sonship is a powerful process. It goes back to the beginning of biblical history and particularly encompasses the story of Elijah and Elisha. Sonship is involved in leadership growth, succession, and inheritance. Sonship doesn't happen instantly. Even in the natural, a son or daughter must grow from the very beginning. From conception to birth takes about nine months. The other lessons that follow take years. However, spiritually speaking, spiritual fathers don't birth our spiritual sons and daughters; we adopt them through the spirit of God. As Romans 8:14-17 says, "For those who are led by the Spirit of God are the children of God. The Spirit you received does not make you slaves, so that you live in fear again; rather, the Spirit you received brought about your adoption to sonship. And by him we cry, *'Abba,* Father.' The Spirit himself testifies with our spirit that we are God's children. Now if we are children, then we are heirs—heirs of God and co-heirs with Christ, if indeed we share in his sufferings in order that we may also share in his glory" (NKJV).

An adoption always goes through a process, too. While not literally, the adoptee is an outcast in the sense of not being part of your natural family. Still, they become a servant, a student, and then a son (or daughter). I am very particular about this because a lot of pastors call people their sons who in turn don't call them their father. I also know of church members who call the pastor their father, but the pastor doesn't call the member their child. Likewise, there are people who say I am their father, but I don't call them my son. So, there must be an agreement between the respective parties, which illustrates the difference between the generic use of "son" and the specific, rich reference.

I understand this distinction because I have been in ministry for a while and know that sometimes pastors use some terms a bit loosely, in a general sense. While there is nothing wrong with that, it helps to understand the more technical definition. A pastor can still call every member their son or daughter, and I understand that is simply a synonym for member.

However, a familiar term should never take the place of one designating a special relationship.

In a very real sense, the greatest men of God will not have more than 12 sons. Jacob had 12 sons, as did Jesus. You are free to call anybody your son until they reject the designation. In the previous two chapters, I talked about servanthood and students, which are the two necessary stages to becoming a son.

There are sons who inherit and sons who don't inherit. Even if you have 12 sons like Jacob, only Judah is going to become the king. You can't have all the sons producing the Messiah; only Judah is qualified to do that. Jesus had 12 disciples, but He only appointed Peter as the leader, although he was later exceeded by Paul. Amongst many sons, one is chosen as the one who inherits. Sometimes great ministries make a transition, but the ministry goes down the drain. When the reigns are handed over to somebody else, he or she kills it.

Law of Inheritance

The fact a ministry flounders under a successor may mean several things: The founder made a bad choice, the successor wasn't adequately prepared, or the ministry was already in decline and without the founder's presence, the weaknesses came to the surface. Whatever the reason, it pays to look at the biblical law of inheritance. Deuteronomy 21:15-17 says:

"If a man has two wives, one loved and the other unloved, and they have borne him children, both the loved and the unloved, and if the firstborn son is of her who is unloved, then it shall be, on the day he bequeaths his possessions to his sons, that he must not bestow firstborn status on the son of the loved wife in preference to the son of the unloved, the true firstborn. But he shall acknowledge the son of the unloved wife as the firstborn by giving him a double portion of all that he has, for he is the beginning of his strength; the right of the firstborn is his" (NKJV).

Note this law is protecting the father from himself. Why? The law says the inheritance is to go to the firstborn, which is particularly applicable when a father must choose who inherits his possessions. The father cannot use his love for a favored child to determine who receives the most. God's Word makes the choice for him. The principle is: The inheritance goes to the one who qualifies, not the child Dad loves the most. Sometimes the beloved son can be a crook, yet even though he isn't qualified, the father passes on a lion's share of his inheritance to that son because the father loves him the most.

This passage says the inheritance is by qualification. In the same way, people in ministry have to follow the process to be qualified. Biology is not the basis; you start as a servant and then become a student. Only then can you qualify as a son and be in line for the inheritance. Just as David did, you must kill your bear and lion before you face your Goliath. There is no easy way to the inheritance. Second Kings 2:9-10 says, "So it was when they had crossed over, that Elijah said to Elisha, 'Ask! What may I do for you before I am taken away from you?' Elisha said, 'Please let a double portion of your spirit be upon me.' So he said, 'You have asked a hard thing. Nevertheless, if you see me when I am taken from you, it shall be so for you; but if not it shall not be so'" (NKJV).

In other words, Elijah was telling Elisha everything he had done until then was not an ironclad guarantee he would see his request granted. The happy conclusion to the story appears in verses 11-15:

"Then it happened, as they continued on and talked, that suddenly a chariot of fire appeared with horses of fire, and separated the two of them; and Elijah went up by a whirlwind into heaven. And Elisha saw it, and he cried out, 'My father, my father, the chariot of Israel and its horsemen!' So he saw him no more. And he took hold of his own clothes and tore them into two pieces. He also took up the mantle of Elijah that had fallen from him and went back and stood by the bank of the Jordan. Then he took the mantle of Elijah that had fallen from him, and struck the water, and said, 'Where is the Lord God of Elijah?' And when he also had struck the water, it was divided this way and that; and Elisha crossed over. Now when the sons of the prophets who were

from Jericho saw him, they said, 'The spirit of Elijah rests on Elisha.' And they came to meet him, and bowed to the ground before him" (NKJV).

The Seven Factors

With his teacher, Elijah, Elisha demonstrated both humility: "I want what you have"—and ambition: "I want a double portion." Elisha aspired to greatness. We are going to look at seven factors that shaped this final phase of the walk of Elijah and Elisha.

Factor 1

The first thing to consider is Elisha's petition for a double portion of Elijah's spirit. Not his works, the results he saw, or the actions he took, but his spirit. Elisha is not looking for outward manifestations but inward qualities. In other words, he is seeking twice as much spiritual capacity, passion, and grace. Elisha doesn't want to do twice the miracles; he wants a double helping of Elijah's spirit, mindset, wisdom, character, and temperament. Often people will seek double the results without desiring the qualities that produced the results. The spirit inside is what produces the action in the natural. Elisha didn't ask for twice the natural; he wanted double of the source of production.

Factor 2

The second thing to look at is Elisha's pursuit. What he is supposed to pursue and what he had to pursue came from a challenge that Elijah gave him: "If you see me, go." Elijah was telling Elisha that is what he had pursue—to keep his eyes on Elijah and the process when Elijah departed. It means Elisha had to keep his focus on Elijah, since there would be many distractions.

While Elijah and Elisha are walking together, I'm not sure what distance lies between them, although I assume it was a normal human pace. They're talking, and then they see chariots of fire. I don't know about you, but when you are talking to somebody and hear a nearby police siren, for a moment you take your eyes off the person to look at the source of the sound. But these weren't any ordinary flashing lights. They were chariots of fire. I don't know about you, but if I were Elisha, I probably would have looked at the chariots of fire. It is only natural to take your eyes off a man to look at a spectacular occurrence.

So the chariots of fire come to separate them and—as that is happening—there is a whirlwind. Scripture says Elijah went up, and if you were looking at the chariots of fire, you would miss the whirlwind. That is the key movement. The chariots of fire represented the diversion, because the whirlwind is what is taking him up to heaven. Elisha saw it because he didn't lose focus, keeping his eye on Elijah. He had to recognize the moment of Elijah's elevation. A son only steps into what the father steps out of; if you do not see what the father steps out of, you do not see what you have to step into. As your father takes up the new, you go and step into the old because that is where the mantle lies.

Factor 3

Third is Elisha's passion. When he sees Elijah go up, he cries out, "My father, my father" (2 Kings 2:12, NKJV). He could have said something like, "My blessing my blessing," "My favour, my favour," "My breakthrough, my breakthrough," or "My hour, my hour." While he had a variety of options of vocabulary, he only chose one relationship—that of father. He didn't care about what big things he was going to do, he just cared about the relationship. Elijah departed, and Elisha stepped into it.

Factor 4

The next thing to notice is Elisha's preference. This is one of the most profound things he did. He took hold of his own clothes and tore them into two pieces. He didn't put on his clothes; he cast aside his own identity. For many people, this would signal the time to put on their own garment. They see the departure of their leader as a time for them to assert themselves. Elisha saw the opposite. He saw the departure of Elijah as a time to cast aside his identity: "This is not my moment to shine; this is the moment for me to elevate Elijah." If you want to know how loyal people are to you, check what they do when you are not in or the garment they wear when you are not around.

Factor 5

Then there is Elisha's promotion. He took the mantle of Elijah. The son takes on the father's responsibilities. Now remember, Elijah did not instruct Elisha to put on his mantle; he didn't even tell him what that meant. The mantle dropped when he was going up because where he was going, he didn't need a mantle. Elijah did not tell Elisha what to do with it. Instinctively, Elisha tore his own garments so he could put on Elijah's garments. I can just hear Elisha saying, "I am not standing in my own office now. I am standing in the office of Elijah. I am honoring Elijah. I am showcasing Elijah."

That was his promotion, and when the transference took place, I believe that was when Elisha was anointed to fulfil the word God gave to Elijah to go and anoint Elisha in his place. It didn't come from pouring on of oil or laying on of hands. It was the servant, student, and son who qualified himself. When the mantle dropped, he didn't leave it on the ground. Instead, he picked it up, tore his own garment, and put on the mantle. Elisha didn't wear it on top of his own clothes or say, "I am my own man now; I've added Elijah to it." No, he took out Elisha and put on Elijah.

Factor 6

Elijah's power became Elisha's. Elisha asked a remarkably interesting question when he took on the mantle, stood by the bank of the Jordan River, did exactly what Elijah had done, and asked, "Where is the Lord God of Elijah?" Wow, the man is gone, and you're asking, "Where is the God of Elijah?" This might be the time for you to ask, "Where is my God?" But what Elisha is saying is, "The source of my power is the source of Elijah's power; the God of Elijah is my God."

Now, for all of you who think you have sons or daughters in ministry, do you have anyone who will behave this way in the future after you are gone? If you don't, then you have to be patient and grow a proper son. A scavenger is the one who eats hungrily after the father has died; a son is the one that takes up his father's mantle. For all of you who are seeking to be sons and daughters—check your heart.

Factor 7

What is the proof of the ministry? Interestingly, it came from his competitors: "The spirit of Elijah rests on Elisha." For a competitor to say this after they were teasing and mocking you just yesterday, but now recognizes you carry the genuine stuff? They are the proof of your ministry. So Elisha starts his ministry not where Elijah began, but where Elijah took off. He starts on a high level, and in so many ways, Elisha did more miracles than Elijah. Some of the miracles were quite similar and took place in almost the same sequence. Others were quite different.

Elisha did more in quantity. When we ask for a double portion, it is not so we would display our greatness to our father or surpass him to show that we can do better. It's to honor him and endorse him, to know that which we inherited from him has done far more in our lives. All of it goes back to Him, our Father, the God of Elijah. Are you ready to put all your success at your Father's feet? Are you ready to say everything you have is His? Are you ready to name your success after Him? I know many people who call themselves sons, but in reality, they are building their own empires and not to the benefit and the glory of their spiritual father or heavenly Father.

The Birthing Process

Sonship is a serious, heavy relationship and is not to be taken lightly. Once you are a son or daughter, even your name is your father's name. Every honor you have goes to the one whose name you carry. Most generations today are fatherless people, but we need more fathers and sons like Elijah and Elisha. We have an obligation not to carry what we have to the grave. We must pass it on and work hard to do so. We must groom sons and put them through the process of becoming a servant and then a student before they become a son.

Remember, the process takes seven steps:
1) Petition
2) Pursuit
3) Passion
4) Preference
5) Promotion
6) Power
7) Proof

As one chord in God's fivefold ministry, if you want a continuity of your legacy, raising up sons and daughters (whether biological or spiritual) is of great essence. Inheritance is given to sons and daughters. Continuity of legacy is given to the firstborn (who is a true son). When everything you build and accomplish in your lifetime crumbles—in other words, falls apart at your demise—then you have failed in your leadership.

Like Elijah passed his mantle to Elisha, Moses passed his mantle to Joshua, Jesus passed His mantle to the 12 disciples, and Paul passed his mantle to Timothy, we need to pass our mantle to our true son or daughter. As leaders of the fivefold ministry, let's create a shift in our thinking and have a kingdom mindset in ministry. May you be mindful of your future rather than your present while using your present as a launchpad for your future. I wish a heartfelt success to all who desire to begin the journey of spiritual fathering and spiritual sonship.

Endnotes

1. "SA's orphan rate on the decline," *Cape Times*, November 22, 2018, https://www.iol.co.za/ capetimes/news/sas-orphan-rate-on-the-decline-18229501#:~:text=%E2%80%9CIn%202017%20there%20 were%202.8,after%20which%20the%20trend%20reversed.

2. Thalia Holmes, "A Helping Hand for the Young and Forsaken," *U.S. News & World Report*, August 8, 2019, https://www.usnews. com/news/best-countries/articles/2019-08-08/ south-africa-struggles-to-care-for-abandoned-babies

3. "Fatherlessness," *Shiloh*, August 7, 2019, https://www. shiloh.org.za/fatherlessness/#:~:text=South%20Africa%20 has%20one%20of,18%20live%20without%20their%20 father.

4. "The Proof Is In: Father Absence Harms Children," *National Fatherhood Initiative*, https://www.fatherhood. org/father-absence-statistic, accessed August 27, 2020.

5. "Fatherlessness."

6. "Follower Quotes," *Good Reads*, https://www.goodreads. com/quotes/tag/follower#:~:text=%E2%80%9CDon't%20 waste%20your%20time,%2C%20success%2C%20and%20 accomplishment.%E2%80%9D&text=%E2%80%9CThe%20 student%20spoke%3A%20Master%2C,follow%20you%20 like%20a%20shadow.

7. Philip Lake Sinitiere, "From the Oasis of Love to Your Best Life Now: A Brief History of Lakewood Church," *Houston History*, Volume 8, Number 3, October 2011, https://houstonhistorymagazine.org/wp-content/ uploads/2011/10/lakewood.pdf.

8. Allison Kugel, "Joel Osteen on coronavirus, Kanye West and keeping the faith," *Church Executive*, April 9, 2020, https://churchexecutive.com/archives/joel-osteen-on-coronavirus-kanye-west-and-keeping-the-faith.

CPSIA information can be obtained
at www.ICGtesting.com
Printed in the USA
BVHW060039030222
627785BV00013B/2124